NLP: THE ESSENTIAL HANDBOOK FOR BUSINESS

Communication Techniques to
Build Relationships, Influence Others,
and Achieve Your Goals

By Jeremy Lazarus

CAREER
PRESS

Pompton Plains, NJ

NLP: THE ESSENTIAL HANDBOOK FOR BUSINESS
Cover design by Rob Johnson/Toprotype
Printed in the U.S.A.

To order this title, please call toll-free 1-800-CAREER-1 (NJ and Canada: 201-848-0310) to order using VISA or MasterCard, or for further information on books from Career Press.

The Career Press, Inc.
220 West Parkway, Unit 12
Pompton Plains, NJ 07444
www.careerpress.com

Library of Congress Cataloging-in-Publication Data

Lazarus, Jeremy.
    [NLP for business success]
    NLP : the essential handbook for business : communication techniques to build relationships, influence others, and achieve your goals / Jeremy Lazarus.
        pages cm
    Revised edition of the author's NLP for business success.
    Includes bibliographical references and index.
    ISBN 978-1-60163-341-5 (paperback) -- ISBN 978-1-60163-435-1 (ebook)
    1. Communication in management--Psychological aspects. 2. Neurolinguistic programming. 3. Success in business--Psychological aspects. I. Title.

HD30.3.L393 2015
658.4'5--dc23
                                                                    2014021299

Acknowledgments

There are several people who I would like to thank. This is in no order of merit.

My colleague Dr. Sally Vanson, for her feedback.

All the founders and subsequent developers of NLP. The many people who have taught me NLP, especially (in alphabetical order) Shelle Rose Charvet, Robert Dilts, John Grinder, Tad James, Ian McDermott, David Shephard, Suzi Smith, Lisa Wake, and Wyatt Woodsmall (apologies for any omissions).

My students and clients, whose willingness to learn and develop is an inspiration to me.

My colleagues Julie, Dave, and Usha, who looked after my business whilst I was writing *NLP: The Essential Handbook for Business*.

Authors of the books referred to in *NLP: The Essential Handbook for Business*.

Jon Finch, Holly Ivins, and Hugh Brune at Crimson Publishing, for their encouragement and assistance.

Contents

Foreword

This is an extremely useful book to introduce those working in organizations to the world of applications from Neurolinguistic Programing (NLP). NLP helps us understand how successful people do what they do.

We all need to take our whole person—our mind, body, and spirit—to work and (in the words of Robert Dilts, one of the co-developers of NLP) "to contribute to the creation of a world to which people want to belong." No longer can we be passengers, just turning up, without effecting change in ourselves and our colleagues.

The end of lifelong careers, the turbulent changes caused by downsizing and market economies, the budget cuts in the public sector, the environmental differences caused by remote and home working, technology, and upheaval in domestic relations have all added vast amounts of complexity to the way we juggle our daily lives. The speed of work is not conducive to reflection or creating the energy to take action.

This pragmatic handbook enables us to quickly and easily understand tools and techniques for causing simple changes within ourselves and others, and is full of examples of applications from the organizational world. We can read about both "organizational skills" and "life skills," blending and aligning the two to work holistically with ourselves as a "whole" person.

In the words of Gregory Bateson, "everything is a metaphor for everything else" and we find that NLP is in fact a metaphor for the firmly established and researched psychological practices that Richard Bandler and John Grinder collected together so that we can use them to become successful in all that we do.

Jeremy has simplified the initial work and makes it truly accessible for all.

—Dr. Sally Vanson

Behavioral change consultant, executive coach, and Certified Master Trainer of NLP

Bradford-on-Avon, UK

Introduction

Welcome to *NLP: The Essential Handbook for Business*. Neurolinguistic Programming (NLP) is essentially a series of techniques, tools, and attitudes which help people to improve their results in all areas of life, including business and the workplace. This book has been written to help you to improve your results in your business or career, and to achieve the kind of improvements that tens (and probably hundreds) of thousands of people have experienced throughout the world, either directly from NLP training or from NLP-based coaching.

NLP was originally developed in the mid-1970s by John Grinder, an associate professor of linguistics at UCLA, and Richard Bandler, one of his star pupils. They began to inquire into how excellent communicators differed from other people. These initial projects to find "the difference that makes the difference" led to further inquiry and projects into the mindset of successful people and organizations, and to the development of some of the widely used NLP techniques which we will cover in this book.

Since its early days, NLP has become widely used in many areas of work. NLP is increasingly becoming accepted as a valid work-based tool, and since the early part of the millennium, there have been Master's degrees from UK universities which have NLP as a significant component. Since 2008, there have been academic conferences in the UK where research papers have been presented regarding the effectiveness of NLP.

If you have been on management development, communication, leadership, or sales training courses, you will probably have already had some previous experience of NLP, whether or not NLP was expressly mentioned on the course, because many of these types of courses will incorporate NLP. This book is suitable both for people who have not knowingly been exposed to NLP and for those who have some experience and want to broaden and deepen their knowledge.

The book will include only the necessary theory to help you to be able to use NLP, and will refer to a few links with existing business and management theories; the bulk of the book will be a practical, hands-on guide to skills that you will be able to use for the rest of your career.

You may have already read my other book, *Successful NLP*, which covers the use of NLP in most areas of life. *NLP: The Essential Handbook for Business* looks specifically at how you can use NLP in numerous workplace situations.

Please note that although this book has the word "business" in the title, the contents are equally applicable in not-for-profit sectors. For example, even though public-sector organizations (such as hospitals, local government) may not have a formal "sales" function, they have revenues, targets, budgets, and expenditure like any business, and their staff need to influence and persuade. So if you work in a not-for-profit organization, whenever you see the term "business" in this book, please consider that it means "work" or "the workplace," and is equally relevant to you. The terms "business," "work," "the workplace," and "organizations" will be used interchangeably throughout the book.

How *NLP: The Essential Handbook for Business* is structured

There are six parts of the book, each with its own brief introduction.

Part I provides an essential background and foundation to the material covered in the rest of the book.

Part II covers communication, including the subtle meaning of words, and how to use words to put your message across even more effectively. It also looks at non-verbal communication, which is often even more important than verbal communication.

Part III looks at how to change the way you think and feel (and hence your results), the "nuts and bolts" of NLP. For each topic, you will learn why it is useful, the relevant information about the topic, and how to use it in a variety of work-related areas and activities. I will answer some of the questions that many of my training course delegates typically have about each topic.

Part IV covers gaining even greater insight into, and how to understand, motivate, and influence, people at work.

Part V covers how to use NLP to replicate excellence.

Part VI takes 16 activities in the workplace (for example, recruitment, sales, and decision-making) and summarizes which of the NLP topics covered earlier in the book would be useful to you in those situations. You can use it as a quick reference guide when you are preparing for, or involved in, one of these 16 activities.

In addition, there are appendices listing answers to two specific exercises on language in Chapter 7, information about NLP training courses available should you wish to learn NLP in a supervised environment, a list of resources for further learning, and a glossary.

Practical tips when reading this book

Most chapters have exercises, tips, and brief stories showing how the techniques have been, and could be, used in work situations. It is recommended that you do all of the exercises in order to solidify your understanding of the relevant technique and how you can use it in practice. Most of the exercises have an estimated duration for your guidance.

Each NLP technique included in the book is explained step by step, in sufficient detail so that you can use the techniques effectively in your work. You will probably find it useful to reread some of the processes or refer to them while doing the exercises. Most people learning NLP find that the more they read through and then practice a particular NLP process, the more effectively they are able to use it.

Many of the topics discussed are relevant for individuals and organizations. As you read the book, it is worth remembering that organizations are simply collections of individuals.

Please note that I have changed the names and sometimes genders of the people referred to in the examples in order to preserve client confidentiality.

A quick word on ethics and best practice

NLP coaching techniques are potentially powerful business tools, and are only to be used in a way that is beneficial to all people involved. Although many of the techniques in NLP are used by qualified NLP professionals (Practitioners, Master Practitioners, and Trainers) to assist others to improve their results, *NLP: The Essential Handbook for Business* is written primarily for people to use for themselves and colleagues, as opposed to when coaching others, unless they have other coaching experience or credentials.

Although NLP techniques are increasingly being used by medical professionals, therapists, and counselors, they are not a substitute for professional medical advice, therapy, or counseling if that is what someone needs. If in doubt, I recommend you initially contact your human resources department or medical practitioner or the Association of NLP (*www.anlp.org*).

Part I

The Foundations

Part I provides the foundation and building blocks for the techniques and practices covered in the rest of the book.

Chapter 1 gives an overview of what NLP is, how it originated, and the types of business situations where NLP can help.

Chapter 2 discusses what happens inside every person's head during every single moment at work, looks at why we are all different from each other, and provides some initial ideas about how to communicate even more effectively.

Chapter 3 moves on to the "mindset for success," the key attitudes and beliefs that successful business people have.

Chapter 4 looks at how to set goals in such a way that makes them really achievable.

1

What Is NLP and How Can It Help You?

Overcoming the challenges you face at work

There are numerous challenges in the workplace, both at an organizational level and at an individual level. This chapter seeks initially to identify the main challenges, and then explain what NLP is and how it can help you to overcome them.

Challenges in the workplace

Businesses and other organizations, and the individuals working in them, are facing greater and more complex challenges than before, as the world's economies become more complex and global, and consumers become more discerning and demanding. At an organizational level, some of the key challenges include:

- How to retain your competitive edge.
- How to recruit, retain, and motivate excellent staff.
- How to balance the needs of all the relevant stakeholders.
- How to create leaders of the future.
- How to make sufficient profit/return on investment.
- How to be flexible enough to respond to, and manage, changes in the economy or your business.
- How to manage diversity.

At a more individual level, the challenges include:

- How to achieve the objectives set by the organization in your job description or at your periodic appraisal (assuming you have them).

- How to create a suitable work–life balance.
- How to manage time and priorities.
- How to manage your own career progression.
- How to keep your skills up to date or even ahead of the field.
- How to feel fulfilled at work and find work that aligns with your values.

This book is dedicated to helping both individuals and organizations (i.e. a collection of individuals) overcome the challenges they face. The challenges outlined above often reflect the following 16 activities that influence results at work.

Internal communications (with staff and colleagues):

1. Management of staff.
2. Team building.
3. Leadership.
4. Human resources, recruitment, and interviewing.
5. Training.
6. Coaching.

External communications (with customers, clients, and suppliers):

7. Sales, business development, and account management.
8. Marketing and advertising.
9. Liaison with clients, customers, patients, and other service users.
10. Procurement.
11. Negotiation.
12. Presentations.
13. Resolving conflicts and misunderstandings.

Work processes:

14. Consultancy, including change management.
15. Improved decision-making.
16. Creative problem solving.

Throughout the book you will learn how to use NLP to help you address each of these topics at both an individual and organizational level.

Exercise 1.1

(Approx. 5–15 minutes)

In light of the topics mentioned above, reflect on why you are reading this book, and what you want to achieve from it, both for you individually and, if you have management responsibilities at work, for your organization. For example, you might want to become even better at making sales, managing your staff, or preventing misunderstandings. Please do this exercise thoroughly; making a list of what you want to gain from reading this book will help you focus your attention. For reasons that will become clear later in the book, the more you know what you want and why you want it, the more you will benefit from this book.

What is NLP?

There are various ways of explaining NLP, and many NLP professionals alter the way they explain it depending on the audience. One often-used definition is "how to use the language of your mind (**N**euro**L**inguistic) to change the **P**rogrammers (or **P**atterns) of behavior." Examples of patterns of behavior at work are:

- Feeling nervous (or confident) before meetings or presentations.
- Becoming angry (or showing understanding) with staff for not delivering on time.
- Procrastinating (or being decisive) about making decisions.

Another definition of NLP is "a series of skills, techniques and approaches to help you to achieve your desired outcomes and goals."

Two main reasons why there are various definitions are because there are different ways in which NLP can be used, for example, coaching, sales, management, sport, counselling, health, and education; and because it is still a relatively new profession.

The benefits of NLP

NLP provides a series of techniques, attitudes, and tools to achieve three main benefits in the workplace:

- Improving communication.
- Changing thinking, attitudes, behaviors, and beliefs.
- Replicating excellence.

Let's take each of the benefits outlined above in turn.

Improving communication

You can have brilliant ideas, but if you can't get them across,
your ideas won't get you anywhere.

—Lee Iacocca, former president at Ford Motor Company and Chrysler

At work, you probably communicate with other people most of the day. You also communicate with yourself; for example, if you are nervous before a meeting, you are in some way communicating to yourself that it may not go well (people rarely get nervous at the prospect of a situation going according to plan). NLP provides a series of ways to communicate more effectively with others (such as staff, customers, suppliers, colleagues) and yourself (by changing the way you perceive the situation if you are nervous, in order to become more relaxed). The communication aspects of NLP are specifically covered in Chapters 2, 6, 7, and 15, and, to some degree, communication is covered in every chapter.

Changing thinking, attitudes, behaviors, and beliefs

Most people experience moments of negativity at work (for example, if their promotion application has been turned down or if they have lost an important contract). Sometimes people behave in ways that are not particularly useful, such as procrastinating, showing frustration inappropriately, or not considering other points of view when it would be beneficial to do so. NLP provides a series of "techniques" to assist you to become more positive and adopt useful behaviors instead of unhelpful ones. Chapters 9 to 13 cover some of these techniques, and Chapter 3 covers the empowering attitudes and beliefs usually found in successful people.

Replicating excellence

Whether you would like to replicate excellence at departmental or organizational level (sometimes referred to as benchmarking), replicate excellence in a particular task such as negotiating or managing, or replicate your own excellence in a different situation (for example, if you are excellent at presenting to five people and feel overwhelmed at presenting to 50, what are you doing in the smaller presentation that you could replicate in the larger one?), NLP has a methodology to assist in replicating excellence, which is known in NLP as "modelling." Chapter 16 will cover the key elements of modelling for organizations.

Caveats

Very occasionally I hear someone say that NLP is "manipulative." This is not the case, because whether something is "manipulative" depends on the intention of the user, not on the thing or tool itself. For example, in the vast majority of situations, a computer will be used in a positive and useful way, and very occasionally it can be used for criminal purposes; that is not a criticism of the computer! Like a computer, NLP is a very powerful tool. Based on many years' experience (my own and that of my NLP associates) of using NLP in business, I believe that the best results come from using NLP only to create solutions that work for all stakeholders in the organization.

Finally, as mentioned in the Introduction, NLP is *not* a substitute for therapy or counseling if that is what someone requires.

2

Communication at Work

What really happens when people talk?

I'm a great believer that any tool that enhances communication has profound effects in terms of how people can learn from each other, and how they can achieve the kind of freedoms that they're interested in.
—Bill Gates, founder of Microsoft

In Chapter 1, we mentioned that improving communication is one of the key benefits of NLP. In this chapter, we will take a closer look at communication in the workplace, start discussing why your messages may not always have the desired effect, and look at how you can use NLP to remedy this. Once you have grasped the simple yet profound elements about communication explained in the next section, your ability to understand and influence others at work will increase, and you will be able to use it as a structure for understanding and using the remainder of this book to your advantage.

Overview of communication at work

Diagram 2.1 shows what happens inside the head of every customer, supplier, and colleague, from the most junior to the most senior. Known as "The NLP Communication Model," it explains in overview why there are misunderstandings, and why you could say the same thing to different customers or staff members but receive very different responses. The Communication Model also provides a framework to understand, communicate with, and influence people that we will return to several times in the book. The following description will mention the NLP terminology, with relevant explanations. It will also focus primarily on individual communication, because when communicating in an organization, you are communicating with a collection of individuals, although the organizational implications will be referred to briefly here and in far more depth in later chapters.

Diagram 2.1: NLP Communication Model

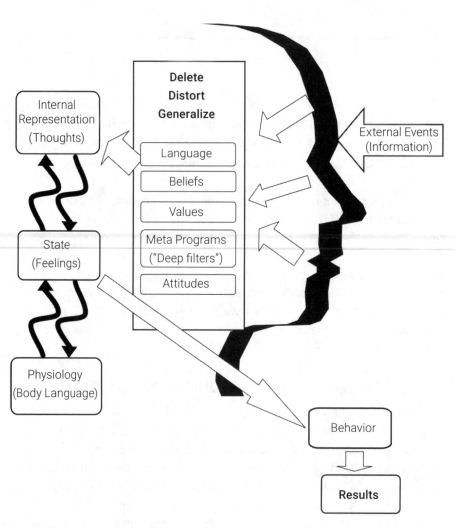

Starting from the top-right-hand side, you receive information from your surroundings, which you perceive through your five senses. This information is then automatically, and almost instantly, filtered (the three key filters are covered in the following section), and leads to an "internal representation" (i.e. a thought or mental image) of what you think you have perceived, usually a combination of pictures, sounds, feelings, internal dialogue, plus possibly taste and smell. Your state (i.e. how you feel) will depend on whether this thought is agreeable to you or not, and this in turn will impact on your physiology—for example, how you are standing, moving, and talking.

These thoughts, feelings, and physiological responses will lead to your behaviors and actions, which ultimately determine the results you achieve. For example, if your boss tells you that you are chairing the meeting in five minutes' time because she has to go to an urgent appointment, and you are having positive thoughts about it, feeling good, and looking and sounding confident, you are more likely to perform better than if you are dreading it, feeling anxious, and stumbling over your words with a faltering voice. Some of the reasons why you might think positively or negatively about the situation will be covered in the section headed "What influences how we filter?" on page 30.

The three main filters

The three main filters are:

- Deletion.
- Distortion.
- Generalization.

Let's take each in turn.

Deletion

When you perceive information, much of it is deleted. It has been estimated that, through our five senses, we receive millions of bits of information each second of the day, whereas our conscious mind can only deal with 126 bits per second (based on work by Professor Mihaly Csikszentmihalyi, author of *Flow*, who estimates that we use 40 bits per second to understand one person speaking to us). Even if these numbers are exaggerated, you are probably not aware of the feeling of this book against your fingertips, nor of the sounds around you, nor of the things in your peripheral vision, until you read these words. Indeed, psychologists assert that if we were aware of all information received by our senses, we would be overwhelmed and would not be able to function. In a positive sense, deleting information helps you to focus on what needs to be done, for example, focusing on specific tasks to meet deadlines. In a less useful sense, deletions can mean that you could miss important information, perhaps because your attention is focused elsewhere. For example, you might be in such a hurry to produce a report that you only skim-read an e-mail containing important information. Please note that deletion is a natural and automatic process, unlike ignoring, which is a conscious choice. Being aware that you delete information can help you to pay closer attention to information that could be important.

Distortion

Distortions are when you assume or interpret information, putting words and labels on an event. So, for example, if your boss's assistant asks you to see him immediately and says that he is not happy, what does this mean? In itself it means nothing, yet you could be excused for having thoughts such as "What have I done wrong?" or "I'm in trouble." Though these thoughts may be appropriate, there are many other possible interpretations of why he wants to see you. Your "negative" assumptions about it will influence how you approach the meeting. If you can learn to recognize your own distortions, you can avoid jumping to conclusions and make more informed decisions and choices.

Generalization

Generalizations are when you take a relatively small amount of information or number of examples and assume that the same supposition applies universally. Used usefully, generalizations help you to learn (e.g. "If I can use one computer, I can use any computer."), and reinforce positive experiences ("I did a good presentation today and last week, so I am a good presenter."). Conversely, they can disempower ("The last few sales meetings went badly—perhaps I'm losing my touch."). As with distortions, if you can learn to recognize your own disempowering generalizations, you will be better able to see situations for what they are and so respond to the situation itself, not your past unhelpful assumptions. Also, disempowering generalizations can lead to unhelpful beliefs; Chapter 13 covers ways to change such beliefs.

Using these three filters at work

Firstly, simply knowing that these filters exist will help you to become more self-aware. Knowing that you delete, distort, and generalize can alert you to the possibility that:

- You may have missed important pieces of information for a project (i.e. deleted), and therefore you may choose to double-check important points.

- If a situation (e.g. interview) has not gone as well as you would have liked, rather than say "it all went wrong" (generalization and possibly distortion), it is worth searching for what went well (i.e. removing your deletions)—for example, that you answered certain challenging questions confidently.

- You could have misinterpreted someone's response, for example, a potential customer not returning your call (distortion). In such situations, it is often useful to ask the person concerned what they meant or how they felt. The worst that can happen is that they confirm your notion, and you can then deal with the reality rather than the possibly inaccurate assumption.

When communicating with others, being aware that they delete, distort, and generalize can help you communicate more effectively. For example, if you are briefing colleagues about an important project, you may want to repeat certain key points or ask them to state in their own words what they believe you have said. This will give you an indication about whether they have deleted or distorted any key points. Similarly, when giving feedback to staff, repeat the key aspects of what they did well and areas for improvement, and ask them to tell you how they are going to do it differently next time.

Tip 2.1

When doing this, be careful not to sound patronizing; asking them to repeat it to make sure *you* have explained *yourself* correctly is probably better than asking them to repeat it to make sure *they* have understood.

What influences how we filter?

There are some additional filters that influence what we delete, distort, and generalize. Let's discuss an overview of each in turn; they will be discussed in more detail in Chapters 6, 7, 8, 13, 14, and 15.

Values

Open your arms to change, but don't let go of your values.
—Dalai Lama

Values can be defined as "what we want/seek," or "what is important to us" in a given situation or context. Each of us has our own unique set of values in life generally, and also in specific contexts, such as work. Examples of life values could be "health" and "financial security for my family"; examples of work values could be "variety" and "progression." Your values are usually reflected in the choices you make and your behaviors, because generally you will make choices that give you more of what is important to you. Organizations also have values, although not necessarily the ones that are espoused in the annual report and accounts or in the laminated copies shown on the wall in the reception area. For example, an organization may say that "respect" is a value, and yet it may not always show respect toward staff and customers: more of this in Chapters 8 and 14.

Values impact the three main filters, because if something is important to you or you are interested in it, you will pay attention to it and delete other information. So a finance director might notice how many people were in a restaurant and make a mental calculation of whether the restaurant is profitable, whereas a fellow diner who happens to be a graphic designer might notice the décor and be oblivious to the number of customers. More generally, do you truly know what is important to your staff, customers, colleagues, and other stakeholders? Chapter 14 covers how to use values in business, for example, to sell more, make better choices, and manage more effectively.

Beliefs

Whether you think that you can, or that you can't, you are usually right.
—Henry Ford, founder of the Ford Motor Company

Beliefs can be defined in several ways, for example:

- Our best current thinking about a topic.
- Those convictions and opinions we hold as being true.

Beliefs can be linked to values, in that you may believe that certain things are important. Whether from the perspective of an individual employee or business owner, beliefs can have a major impact on the results achieved. A salesman who does not believe in the effectiveness of his product, or in his abilities as a salesman, will almost certainly sell less than a salesman who does have empowering beliefs about the product or his abilities.

Linking back to the NLP Communication Model (page 26) and the filters, if we believe something is true, we will often filter out (i.e. delete, distort, or generalize) information that contradicts it so that it fits in with our beliefs. The term "cognitive dissonance," based on the work of Leon Festinger in his 1957 book *A Theory of Cognitive Dissonance*, describes the discomfort or difficulty we experience when we hold two conflicting beliefs, and the subsequent process of changing one of the beliefs to reduce the discomfort. The following example illustrates this.

Story 2.1

One of my corporate clients produces IT software and support. They had been targeting businesses with a turnover of up to $75 million. The company decided to expand and target larger companies, expecting that the success of the sales team would continue. Mark and Julio had been the two leading sales people. However, for six months after the expansion, Julio struggled to sell to the larger clients, and I was asked to coach him. Mark's sales figures were higher than ever.

It became clear in our coaching discussions that Julio held a belief that it would be difficult for him to sell to large companies, because he thought they would be too discerning. Interestingly, Mark believed that it would be *easier* to sell to larger companies, because the buyers were more sophisticated and better able to appreciate the benefits to them of the products. So for both people, there were similar (if not identical) external circumstances ("events"), yet their respective beliefs led to different thoughts and ultimately different results. I worked with Julio to successfully change his beliefs and hence to improve his sales. (Some NLP belief-change techniques are covered in Chapter 13.)

From the Communication Model perspective, Julio's changing his beliefs led to his having more useful internal representations (thoughts), state (feelings), and physiology (body language) before and during sales meetings, which led to his behaviors changing and results improving.

At an organizational level, **beliefs** about, for example, the best way to treat staff will impact on results.

Language

Language shapes the way we think, and determines what we can think about.

—Benjamin Lee Whorf, American linguist

The words that individuals and organizations use impact the listeners/readers (radio advertising would be pointless were this not the case). As an example to demonstrate the impact of language on an individual, consider someone saying the following two sentences to himself:

1. I can't (i.e. am not capable to) do X (negotiate/coach my team/ make good business decisions).

2. I haven't yet learned how to do X (negotiate/coach my team/ make good business decisions) as well as I would like.

For most readers, the first statement leaves little scope for possibility and may leave them feeling disempowered (with consequent negative impact on behaviors and results), whereas the second statement implies, and even creates, possibility and is more empowering. Similarly, from an organization's perspective, a manager speaking to employees (using "you" instead of "I" in the two statements above) will impact those employees negatively or positively, depending on which of the two statements is used.

We will cover ways to use language effectively in Chapters 6 and 7.

Meta programs (deep filters)

"Meta programs" is an NLP term for filters which, in effect, sit beyond, or underpin, other filters. They are deeply embedded filters that operate irrespective of the content of what's happening, and they tend to determine *how* we think as opposed to the other filters previously mentioned, which are more about *what* we think. For this reason, I will also refer to them as "deep filters." It is generally accepted in the field of NLP that there are around 15–20 key deep filters, and this topic will be covered more extensively in Chapter 15.

By way of illustration, let's look at an example of one of the deep filters known as the "direction filter." People can be motivated either "toward" what they want or "away from" what they don't want, or somewhere along the spectrum. The two ends of this particular spectrum are sometimes known in the business world as the "carrot or stick," or "push/pull." For example, someone might be highly motivated and want to achieve their goals and targets because of the material things and kudos they will gain and be able to have (toward), whereas a colleague doing the same job might be highly motivated to avoid failure because they don't want to feel bad, stagnate, or live in a small house like the one they grew up in (away from).

By knowing about our own, and other people's, deep filters, we can gain greater insight into our own, and other people's, behaviors and responses to situations, and therefore be better able to influence individuals and target audiences. Using the example in the previous paragraph, you would motivate the "toward" employee by emphasizing what they would gain or achieve if they completed the task well (such as money, time off in lieu, enhanced promotion prospects), and motivate the "away from" employee by emphasizing the downsides of not completing the task well (such as not getting a pay rise, having to working longer hours, or damaged promotion prospects).

Attitudes and experiences

You can consider "attitude" as a set of beliefs and values about a specific topic. "Experiences" are the events that have happened to us, and link to the other filters to help mould our personality.

"Conscious thinking" versus "automatic pilot"

Before we end this chapter, I would like to say a few words about another important topic related to the Communication Model. In NLP, there is the concept of "conscious mind" and "unconscious" (or "subconscious") mind. An awareness of this will help you to manage your own responses to events at work, and be better able to work with the responses of other people.

In summary, your conscious mind is the "rational" part of your mind and, in a work context, performs business tasks such as target setting, planning, preparing for meetings, and financial calculations.

Your unconscious mind holds the memories, knowledge, experiences, beliefs, values, and emotions, and has different levels. At a superficial level of the unconscious mind, most people are able to retrieve some of their memories and be aware of some of their beliefs and values. At a deeper level, they may not be aware of some of their deeper beliefs and values, and their emotional responses happen automatically. For example, feeling nervous or excited before an important meeting is an automatic (unconscious) response. Julio (Story 2.1 on page 31–32) was not initially consciously aware of his belief about selling to larger companies; our conversations helped bring it to his conscious awareness.

The purpose of mentioning this topic is to raise your awareness that everyone you interact with at work will to some degree be driven by their automatic responses; if all business decisions were based purely on rational (i.e. conscious) motives, it is likely that all procurement staff in different companies within a specific sector would buy from the same supplier, and that people within an organization would agree on most decisions. In reality, people base their decisions to some degree on emotional factors, or deeper beliefs and values, regardless of whether they are consciously aware of it. This awareness, plus the knowledge you will gain from this book, will help you to uncover, for example, the values of your staff and hence be able to influence them more effectively.

Though it is outside the scope of this book to delve deeply into the more automatic (or unconscious) elements, it is important that you are aware of this. If you are interested in learning more, there are numerous books available on the subject of hypnosis, which will give a deeper insight into the unconscious mind. Some of these are listed in the "Resources for Further Learning" section.

Final thoughts

Because we all have different ways in which we use language, beliefs, values, deep filter/meta-program profiles, attitudes, and experiences, it is hardly surprising that we have different opinions and observe different things about a given situation at work, which may sometimes lead to different (and sometimes unexpected) responses from other people. For example, economic forecasts vary depending on the economist, despite the economists having access to the same economic data. Similarly, the strategic direction of an organization may alter when a new chief executive is appointed, despite the two chief executives having access to the same marketing and business data.

Much of the information in this chapter relates to how an individual person thinks. Similar principles apply to the way in which groups and organizations operate; for example, teams and organizations have values and beliefs, which are often referred to as the "culture." This book seeks to improve the degree to which your messages will be received in the way *you* intended, and that you receive the messages from other people in the way *they* intended.

3

Attitudes That Count

The mindset for business success

---

*Success or failure in business is caused more by
mental attitude even than by mental capacities.*
—Sir Walter D. Scott, founder of leading Australian
management consultancy company WD Scott

I often hear people talk about NLP in terms of influencing, communication, and a series of techniques. Rarely do they mention the attitudes and beliefs that underpin NLP. In my experience as a trainer and coach, it is these attitudes that make the biggest difference. Indeed, the senior managers and directors who attend my NLP business-training courses tell me that if the whole of their organization used the material that we will cover in this chapter alone, profits (or efficiencies for not-for-profit organizations) would increase typically by 50 percent. The smallest figure I have heard quoted is 20 percent. So please pay attention!

Setting the scene

As we discussed in Chapter 1, NLP was developed by modeling excellence. The early developers of NLP found that there were certain beliefs and attitudes held by all successful people. These can be grouped into two main areas:

- The NLP Presuppositions. These are a series of assumptions to be adopted when using NLP and form the basis of an ethical framework for using it.

- The Principles for Success. These guide almost all courses of action and can be a useful framework for achieving goals.

We will consider these two main areas in turn.

NLP Presuppositions

There are around 15 NLP Presuppositions; the exact number and specific wording may vary slightly because different schools of NLP have their own approach to training the topic. These NLP Presuppositions are relevant to a wide range of NLP activities, such as coaching, therapy, achieving performance targets, and communication skills. For the purposes of this book, we will consider only those nine Presuppositions that are most relevant to the workplace. For your convenience, these have been divided into three groups (please note that these groupings are for guideline purposes and that some could fall into more than one category).

1. Externally focused, i.e. based on or impacting on the outside world.
2. Internally focused and internal attitudes.
3. Results/activity focused.

Please use common sense when applying these Presuppositions at work, because not all of them will be relevant in every situation.

Externally focused

There are three key NLP Presuppositions in this category:

- Have respect for other people's point of view.
- The meaning and outcome of communication are in the response you get.
- Our interpretation of a situation is not the situation itself.

Have respect for other people's point of view.

Seek first to understand, then be understood.

—Stephen Covey, author of *The 7 Habits of Highly Successful People*

You will appreciate from the Communication Model that each person is unique, with different values, beliefs, meta-program profiles, and experiences. Though you might not agree with your colleague, supplier, or customer, if you can demonstrate that you respect their point of view, you will be more likely to influence them (see Covey's quote), and even if they do not come around to your way of thinking on this particular issue, you can agree to disagree and still maintain a healthy working relationship. Conversely, if you do not demonstrate respect, the relationship may be damaged.

The meaning and outcome of communication
are in the response you get.

The Communication Model shows that everyone filters information differently. Though your words and actions might seem clear to you, people you interact with at work might interpret them differently from how you intended, and therefore might respond differently from how you expected; that is, their response is based on the meaning *they* interpret instead of the one you meant. Therefore, if certain people at work are not responding in the way you expect, instead of expecting *them* to change, it is easier if *you* change the way *you* communicate. Much of this book is focused on how you can be more flexible when communicating.

Our interpretation of a situation is not the situation itself.

The map is not the territory.

—Alfred Korzybski, philosopher and scientist,
who developed the theory of general semantics

It is rare for any meeting to take place where everyone agrees with each other, and then all take the actions exactly as everyone at the meeting expects. This is because we all have our own unique interpretation of events, and this interpretation is not the event. Therefore, you will interpret a situation, such as a negotiation, in a different way from someone else, and you might describe it, for example, as a "battle," whereas for someone else it is just a conversation or an exploration. We all respond to our own map of the event, not to the actual territory. NLP can help you to appreciate other perspectives (see Chapter 11) and ask questions to gain deeper understanding (see Chapter 7).

Internally focused and internal attitudes

There are three key NLP Presuppositions in this category:

- There is no failure, just feedback.
- Flexibility goes a long way.
- We are, or can learn to be, in charge of our mind and therefore our results.

There is no failure, just feedback.

Failure is only the opportunity to begin again, only this time more wisely.
—Henry Ford, founder of the Ford Motor Company

There are so many examples of successful business people who "failed" before becoming successful that this book could be devoted to just this topic. Examples include:

- Rowland Hussey Macy Sr., the founder of Macy's department-store chain, who had at least four retail failures.
- Thomas Edison, the holder of over 1,000 patents in the U.S. alone, who allegedly made 10,000 attempts before successfully creating the light bulb.
- Bill Gates (the founder of Microsoft), who co-ran a business called Traf-O-Data in the 1970s which lost money.
- Walt Disney, whose Laugh-O-Gram Films business went bankrupt after around one year's trading.

The moral is simple. There is no failure, merely feedback that what you have done did not work. Learn from it, retain (or even intensify) your motivation, and move forward. NLP can help you set goals and maintain the motivation to achieve them (see Chapters 4, 8, and 14).

Flexibility goes a long way.

*Insanity: doing the same thing over and over again
and expecting different results.*
—Albert Einstein

Following on from the previous Presupposition, if what you are doing is not working, it makes sense to adjust your approach in some way. If your approach to getting a job interview (or an appointment, sale, or promotion) is not succeeding yet, alter your approach. Sometimes, being willing and able to be very flexible is important, as the following story illustrates.

Story 3.1

Napoleon Hill, a highly successful businessman and author of *Think and Grow Rich*, recounts that he got his first job by writing to a prospective employer that he really wanted to work for, congratulating the owner (to whom he sent the letter) because he (Hill) had chosen that organization to be his first employer, and so happy would they be with his abilities that he would be willing to work for nothing for a specified period of time with the proviso that when they hired him they would reimburse him for his previous work.

We are, or can learn to be, in charge of our mind and therefore our results. Even if you feel nervous about certain situations (interviews, selling, presentations, meetings with senior people), or have limiting beliefs about your capabilities, you can learn to change the way you think and therefore change your results. NLP has several techniques to help you feel at your best, some of which are covered in this book (particularly Chapters 10 and 13).

Results/activity focused

There are three key NLP Presuppositions in this category:

- People have all the potential that they need to make the changes they want.
- People are making the best choices they believe they have available and are doing the best they can.
- Modeling excellence leads to improved performance.

*People have all the potential that they need
to make the changes they want.*

The past does not equal the future.

—Tony Robbins, motivational speaker, author, and performance coach

Following on from the previous Presupposition, it is useful to consider that each of us has untapped potential. So whether you are thinking about yourself and your own aspirations, or managing staff and their aspirations, recognizing that everyone has abilities to learn, adapt, be motivated, and excel in certain circumstances will help you (and your colleagues) to progress further than if you believe that everyone is limited to their previous results. The key point here is that though not everyone can be the most successful business person in the world, the past does not equal the future, and NLP has many techniques to help people fulfil their potential and progress further than they otherwise would.

People are making the best choices they believe they have available, and are doing the best they can. Sometimes other people's choices and behaviors at work may seem counterproductive when viewed by an outsider: examples could include repeatedly being late for meetings, getting "angry," or being "obstructive" at brainstorming sessions. Though commercial reality and common sense would suggest that prolonged and continued unhelpful behavior should not be tolerated, sometimes it can be useful to recognize that each person is making the choices that they believe are best for them at the time, given their awareness of the available range of behaviors. This awareness can help you gain greater understanding of your colleagues and, if appropriate, help coach them to make more useful choices. For example, someone frequently being late might be due to their having a belief that being early or on time is a waste of their own time because other people are usually late, and so they squeeze in extra work to try to be productive. Helping them to see the impact on others (see Chapter 11 in particular) might help you to raise their awareness and hence change their behavior.

Modeling excellence leads to improved performance.

"Modeling," that is, observing, analyzing, and replicating excellence, is how NLP was initially developed. In a work context, benchmarking (i.e. comparing your processes and results to those of a similar organization or process) is a widely accepted method of improving performance, usually at an organizational level. Benchmarking successful individual performance is something that usually improves individual (and hence business) results. For example, what are the key aspects of the beliefs, attitudes, and behaviors of outstanding managers, sales people, and customer-service professionals that differentiate them from their colleagues who are merely good? In Chapter 16 we will discuss further how to model excellent performance.

Being "At Cause"

Shallow men believe in luck; strong men believe in cause and effect.

—Ralph Waldo Emerson, essayist, lecturer, poet, and philosopher

The NLP Presuppositions can be summarized by the concept of "cause and effect." "Cause and effect" means that for every "effect" there is an underlying "cause"; for example, the economic circumstances (effect) are caused by decisions made by governments, consumers, businesses, etc. Extending this concept to the workplace, people can either be "At Effect" or "At Cause." People who have an At Effect mindset tend to exhibit the following behaviors:

- Complaining.
- Making excuses.
- Being negative.
- Expecting others to make things good for them.
- Blaming circumstances (i.e. "causes").

People who have an At Cause mindset tend to:

- Have a "can do" attitude.
- Be positive.
- Take responsibility for their own actions and results.
- Take action to achieve what they want despite circumstances so that they impact the circumstances rather than the circumstances impacting them.

In the numerous NLP work-based training courses I have run, this one topic leads to almost total agreement that being At Cause leads to better results for individuals, teams, and organizations.

Exercise 3.1

(approx. 1 minute)

On a scale of 0 to 100 percent, where 100 percent means you are fully At Cause and 0 percent means you are fully At Effect, estimate where you are on the cause-effect spectrum. Please be honest with yourself.

So even in the face of adversity at work, such as poor sales figures, low economic growth, and corporate restructuring, if you have an At Cause mindset, you will produce better results than if you have an At Effect mindset. By putting into practice the information covered throughout this book, you will increase your At Cause score.

The Principles for Success in business

There is an NLP model known as the Principles for Success. The model has six elements. Let's take each in turn.

- **Know what you want.** Before starting any work activity, ranging from a simple meeting to a major corporate restructuring, know what you want (your goal or desired outcome). Chapter 4 covers goal setting in some detail.

- **Take feedback.** Are you on track to achieve your goal? (Chapter 5 provides some pointers on gaining "in the moment" feedback from individuals.) If you are not on track, then....

- **Be flexible.** Referring back to one of the NLP Presuppositions (Flexibility goes a long way) and the quote from Einstein, if something is not working in the way you want, make changes.

- **Build and maintain good relationships.** In NLP, we call this "rapport," and this is covered in Chapter 5.

- **Have a positive mental attitude.** The fundamentals of having a positive mental attitude have been covered in this chapter, and this book provides various NLP techniques (covered in Part

III) to assist you to have a positive mental attitude, and to help you help others to have the same.

- **Take action.** Without action, nothing changes. The NLP Presuppositions, being At Cause, and the Principles for Success offer individuals, teams, and organizations a set of distinctions that leads to significantly better results. Here is an exercise that I do on all of my business-training courses.

Exercise 3.2

(approx. 10 minutes)

Think of two (or more) situations at work that went well, and two (or more) that did not go well. For those that went well, notice to what extent you were using the NLP Presuppositions, the At Cause mindset, and the Principles for Success, even if you didn't know about this at the time. For those situations that did not go well, notice which of these would have been useful had you known about them at the time. Examples could be customer or supplier meetings, presentations, interviews, or dealing with a difficult client or patient. On my training courses, I ask people to discuss this in small groups (adding around 10–20 minutes to the exercise).

4

Achieving Your Goals

How to set and reach your targets

Goals are the fuel in the furnace of achievement.
—Brian Tracy, author, entrepreneur, and motivational speaker

The first Principle for Success (Chapter 3) is to set goals and to know what you want. In this chapter, we will cover the importance of setting goals effectively, how to do so in the workplace for both individuals and organizations, and how to apply the principles of goal setting at work.

Exercise 4.1

(approx. 5 minutes)

Set at least one work-related goal. Ideally, have a short-term, medium-term, and long-term goal. For example, your short-term goal might be to pass your next set of professional exams, a medium-term goal might be to become qualified (lawyer, accountant, surveyor, nurse), and a long-term goal could be to start your own business/agency. If you run your own business, or are senior enough to set departmental or organizational goals, then set goals for your organization and a work goal for you. We will refer to these later in the chapter.

Why set goals?

A more relevant question here is "Why set goals using the principles outlined in this chapter?" This is because most people in the business world are already accustomed to setting goals. Every organization I have heard of will have targets, set budgets, and have strategic plans that are quantified, in order to focus the efforts of all staff on the same organizational goals and against which to monitor and compare progress. Most individuals working in these organizations will have goals, targets, and objectives set at least annually at their performance review and appraisal.

Also, from a personal psychological point of view, having a clearly defined goal or target will help your "reticular activation system" (i.e. the brain's internal radar) to focus on finding and selecting relevant information (from the millions of available bits of information—see page 27–28) that will help you achieve your goals. As outlined in the Principles for Success in Chapter 3, once you have a clear goal, you can then start the journey towards achieving it.

The additional benefits of setting goals using NLP principles are as follows:

- It provides real clarity on what the individual or group wants.
- It helps ensure that the goals are truly what the individual and organization want. This is particularly relevant for smaller businesses, where the goals are often an extension of, or related to, the owner's goals.
- Consequently, this ensures that individuals and business don't waste time, effort, and energy in aiming for a goal that would not be appropriate, probably only realizing the goal was not appropriate after many hours of effort and much expense.

It is important to make clear that the goal-setting process is separate from actually achieving it. So, for example, if you are a manager coaching a member of staff at her annual appraisal, my suggestion is that you agree on the goal before beginning to coach her on how to achieve it. Chapter 17 touches on the use of NLP when coaching.

A sports approach to achieve business goals

Nowhere is goal setting more widely embraced than in the area of sport, and there are some aspects of goal setting that business can learn from sport. Within the world of sport, it is generally accepted that there are three types of goals:

- Outcome goals (the "why").
- Performance goals (the "what").
- Process goals (the "how").

Outcome goals relate to the big picture, the overall aim, the goal that really motivates and provides the "why." Examples in sport could be winning the Olympic Gold or, for mere mortals, winning the local tennis or golf tournament. In the workplace, this might relate to, for example:

- Taking your company into the Fortune 500 top companies.
- Having your organization in the top quartile of a specific measure, such as a certain type of healthcare service or employee satisfaction.
- Being the top performing sales person this quarter.
- Getting a promotion this year.

Though outcome goals are, almost by definition, motivating, they are not always within the control of the person or organization. This is where performance goals are useful.

Performance goals relate to the measures that will need to be achieved to give you or your organization the best chance of success (i.e. "what" needs to be achieved). An athlete could run the race of their life, yet if someone performs better, they won't win the gold. Similarly, a business could produce excellent profits but if other companies do better, that business might not achieve its outcome goals (using the examples above). Examples of performance goals, relating to the examples used previously, could be:

- Produce pre-tax profits of $300 million this year.
- Have staff turnover of 12 percent.
- Close $1.5 million of business this quarter.
- Have the new computer system go live this year.

These performance goals are something tangible to aim for, and will be something within your control or that of the organization. And although these goals are "what" you will be aiming for, they do not identify "how" you will do it.

Process goals relate to the specifics of "how" you or your organization will achieve the performance goals, which in turn will provide the best chance of achieving the outcome goals. Just as an athlete will have a whole raft of specific tasks and measures, such as doing 100 push-ups daily or working on a specified technical aspect of their sport, so you or your business will have specific process goals such as:

- Create three new products or expand into a new geographic area.
- Introduce employee-engagement surveys or introduce semi-annual rather than annual appraisals.
- Make a presentation at the annual conference for your industry or make 25 cold calls each day.
- Do the initial user test this month or migrate one subset of the system within three months.

Tip 4.1

When setting goals, be aware of the distinction between the three categories. As a guide, outcome goals tend to be longer term, performance goals are medium term, and process goals are short term.

In some situations, the distinction between outcome and performance goals, and between performance goals and process goals, can be blurred. Therefore, use these three categories to inform you, rather than spend too much energy debating which category a goal fits into.

NLP approaches to goal setting

Within the field of NLP, there are several models for goal setting, all of which are complementary and lead to the creation of what is known as a "well-formed goal" or "well-formed outcome" (in NLP, the terms *outcomes* and *goals* are often used interchangeably). A well-formed goal/outcome is one that is formulated in a way that significantly increases the likelihood of the goal being achieved because of the clarity, desirability, and appropriateness of the goal. These goal-setting models usually consist of a series of questions to ask when setting goals and/or a checklist of conditions to be met for goals to be considered "well-formed." The benefit of using this approach when setting goals was covered in "Why set goals?" (page 48).

Although these two models are extremely useful (particularly for general use by individuals or when they are not totally clear on what they want), in the business world the use of SMART objectives/goals is more widely used. The NLP goal-setting models can be adapted into the SMARTER method (an extension of SMART goals). Because of these factors we will be using the SMARTER method here.

Please note that the information that follows will greatly extend the effectiveness and your knowledge of the traditional SMART model (there are 15 points rather than the commonly used five or six), so please approach this with fresh eyes.

The following explanation of the SMARTER model will be a general description, mainly for individuals, followed by some specifics about how it can be used individually at work or with groups and organizations. Although we will take each point in the SMARTER model separately, as you will see, some of the points relate to each other. With some of the points that follow, I mention useful questions (italicized) that will help you incorporate that point into the goal(s) you set. In order to make the SMARTER points clear, let's use the following goal as an example.

It is October 31, 20XX (specific date, 18 months in the future), and my advertising business, based in central Paris, which I formed last year has made $1,000,000 of sales, with a pre-tax profit of $150,000 after a $75,000 salary each to me and my business partner (named). We have an order book of $350,000 for the next 10 weeks, and forecast turnover for the following 12 months is $1,500,000 and forecast profit is $400,000 after a $100,000 salary each. I have worked on average 50 hours per week, and have a good work–life balance and time for my family, my health and fitness, and my social life.

S

Specific. Be specific about what the goal is. Say exactly and specifically what you want. Some of my course delegates say that their goal is to make more money. When I give them one penny, they have achieved their stated goal, yet is it what they actually want?

What will you be seeing, hearing, feeling, saying to yourself, and even tasting and smelling when you achieve your goal? The more sensory specific you can be, the more likely it is that you will achieve the goal. In the example above, you would want to ascertain exactly how you would know that the sales, profit, and salary goal had been achieved, and that the second year's targets were likely to be met. If relevant, you might also want to ask questions such as "Where, when, how, and with whom do you want this?" In this example, the answers are central Paris, the specified date, advertising business, and the name of your business partner.

Simple. As far as possible, state what you want as simply and briefly as possible. This is not to say that it will be simple to achieve it. Stating it simply gives all those involved the greatest likelihood of understanding it rather than deleting or distorting the information, or getting overwhelmed by a rambling description of the goal.

Tip 4.2

Ask yourself whether an intelligent and informed child could understand your goal. If so, it is probably specific and simple enough.

M

Measurable. This links to "specific" above. Make sure the goal is measurable, ideally with numbers or amounts included. Some of my clients say that their goal is to be "more successful." Though this is a nice idea, how would this be measured? *How would you know **undeniably** when you had it?* In the example goal, it might be that you would be seeing the annual financial statement or hearing your accountant tell you the financial results. There are also stated amounts of money and a number of hours.

Meaningful and motivating. The more meaningful and motivating the goal is to you, the more likely it is that you will do what it takes to achieve it. Does the goal give you more of what you want, that is, your values (Chapter 14)? *What will this outcome get for you or allow you to do?* In this example, having your own business might be a lifetime's ambition, and it might help you to do other things in your life such as buy the house you want and give you the independence you want.

Maintainable (by you). It is important that you can make it happen yourself or take steps to make it happen—for example, if you are a manager or owner, managing your staff to make the goal happen. If you are totally reliant on other people, and if you have little direct influence over them, either the goal is less likely to be achieved or you will need to take this into account when designing and planning the goal and steps to achieve it.

More than one way to achieve it. Most goals can be achieved in various ways. It is worth being aware that if there is only one way to achieve it, and for whatever reason that way becomes blocked, then the goal becomes far more difficult to achieve, so it is best to choose a goal where there is more than one way to achieve it. In practice, most goals can be achieved in many ways. Using the example, there is a wide variety of companies that use advertising services, and a wide variety of advertising mediums.

A

Achievable. It is essential that you believe that your goal is achievable. Research has shown that the most motivating goals are those that the person believes that they can achieve, even though it may be a challenge. If you believe that the goal is not achievable, it is unlikely that you will put much effort into trying to achieve it. Two useful questions to ask are *Has someone in a broadly similar situation (to you) achieved something broadly similar?* and *Have you ever had or done something like this before?*

If the answers are yes, it suggests that the goal is achievable. Remember, even if the answers are no, there are frequently groundbreaking achievements in the workplace due to, for example, technological advancements.

It is also useful to ask, "Where are you now in relation to your goal?" If you are too far away, perhaps you need to adjust your goal, for example, by adjusting the target date.

Tip 4.3

Remember Napoleon Hill's story (page 41) about having a definite purpose and a burning desire to achieve it. If you really want something, even if it hasn't been achieved before, you're already a long way towards achieving it.

All areas of life. Life coaches would say that it is important to set goals in all areas of your life, in order to create the sort of balanced life you want. From a business coach's perspective, whether or not I ask clients to do this, I would certainly want all my clients to consider the impact of their work goals on other areas of their life, notably their health, relationships, and finances. To the extent that your goal impacts positively on all areas of your life, or at least that there are no significant negative consequences, you will feel more motivated to take action to achieve the goal than if there were significant negative consequences. Using the example, the goal states the work–life aspects.

As if now. According to Napoleon Hill and the many business leaders he interviewed, successful people see their goals as if they were happening now or had already happened. Hill talked about Henry Ford having a picture in his mind of the combustion engine working. Also, many sports champions visualize success already happening before sports events. So when you state and think about your goal, do so as if it were happening now, or has already happened, that is, state it in the present or past tense.

R

Realistic. This will often be linked to "achievable." There is a subtle difference between the two: though it might be technically achievable for a 44-year-old who had never earned more than $50,000 to become a chief executive of a blue-chip company before his 45th birthday, it is almost certainly not realistic.

Right and responsible. This links to "All areas of life" stated previously. Is the goal truly right for you? Are there any significant negative consequences for you or for those close to you if you achieve this goal? Does it fit in with your own sense of who you are? Will this goal keep the positive aspects of the current situation? Will achieving this goal open doors for you and make possible for you other things that you want in your work? *What will this goal get for you or allow you to do?*

Story 4.1

Jane was working with a relatively small, niche healthcare business whose goal for the previous three years was to become the leading company in their industry within six months. They had made relatively little progress. When she asked them to name a specific date and work toward that, the whole company had something to focus on, and they achieved as much in three months as they had in the previous three years.

T

Timed (and dated). It is essential to specify a date and, if appropriate, a time of day (for example, hearing about exam results) for your goals. "Within three months" is not a date and is often not effective because there is no specific target to move toward. October 31, 20XX (stated year) is a date.

Toward. Although appearing last on the traditional SMART goal list, this is potentially the most important item. Stating what you want, without any comparisons (such as "more" or "less"), as opposed to what you don't want, helps you focus on what you do want. Based on recent developments in quantum physics, there is evidence supporting the assertions and findings of people such as Napoleon Hill that our thoughts manifest into reality. For example, if you think about not wanting to do badly at the interview, the thought in your mind is "do badly at the interview." It is much more effective to think about doing well at the interview. Therefore, state your goals in terms of what you want to be, do, or have. *What specifically do you want?*

Tip 4.4

Say it how you want it to be!

E

Ecology. An important topic in NLP is that of "ecology." In NLP, ecology relates to the consequences of actions on you and all areas of your life (such as health, money, relationships, family, hobbies), people around you, and society in general. This links to "Right and responsible" and "All areas of life."

To the extent that your goals are truly right for the three groups above, you will receive support from, or at least not be obstructed by, people in your life. Though in the short term people are sometimes willing and able to put up with some negative consequences (such as not spending enough time with family or maintaining fitness) in order to achieve their goals, over the longer term, this is usually not sustainable.

Therefore, when setting goals, please bear in mind the consequences (this relates to "Right and responsible"), that is, what you will gain or lose if you achieve this goal. Here are some additional questions to ask when setting goals, in order to increase the likelihood of the goals being ecological (these will be referred to as "the four ecology questions" later in the book).

1. What will happen if you achieve it?

2. What will happen if you don't achieve it?

3. What won't happen if you achieve it?

4. What won't happen if you don't achieve it? (This is a brain-twister and a very useful question.)

If any of the answers suggest that there are significant negative consequences, or that it is not ecological, to achieve this goal, then consider adjusting your goal or discussing it with the people impacted by your goal.

Story 4.2

Tom, an engineer, wanted to achieve his ambition of running the Iron Man triathlon in Hawaii. The race takes around 10 hours to complete and requires an immense amount of training and preparation. Recognizing that he would have less time for his work, his partner, and his friends and family (i.e. negative consequences), Tom had various conversations and negotiated a four-day week, doing his training with his partner (also a triathlete), and arranged a big party for friends and family for the week after the race to thank them for their patience and support even though he would not have seen much of them recently.

Tip 4.5

Wherever possible and practical, seek to set "win–win" outcomes.

R

Resources. What resources do you have, and what else will you need, in order to achieve the goal? In a business sense, resources relate to things such as money, time, and people. In an NLP context, "resources" can also relate to more inherent personal attributes, such as confidence, experience, determination, ability to focus, and skill levels.

Exercise 4.2

(approx. 10–15 minutes)

If you are used to using the standard SMART model, reflect on the similarities and differences between it and the SMARTER model explained previously. Make a list of the additional areas in the SMARTER model that will be useful to you (and/or your organization), and include them when setting goals in the future.

Examples of SMARTER goals

Here are some other examples of SMARTER goals, including process, performance, and outcome goals. Assuming that all the SMARTER criteria are met, here is how the goals might be worded.

- It is October 31, 20XX (this year), and I have sold $150,000 in the last three months.

- It is January 1, 20XX (two years from now), and I am a qualified accountant.

- It is May 31, 20XX (three years from now) and our organization has won a national award for technological innovation.

- It is March 31, 20XX (this year) and the payroll department that I run has no queries or errors outstanding for longer than three hours.

Goal setting for individuals

The goal-setting principles explained above can be used in several ways for individuals:

- For yourself, setting your own career or business goals and targets.

- When managing or coaching other people around their own career or business goals.

- If you manage people, you can use this at appraisals, or when someone gets promoted into a new role.

Goal setting for groups and organizations

You can use these principles with groups, departments, or organizations, for example:

- When coaching or leading a team, to set the direction and targets.
- Boards of directors or management teams can use these to set longer-term goals as part of a strategic plan.
- During project meetings, especially at the initial stages, setting the direction and target.
- If there is a significant change in direction, plans or circumstances, these principles can help you to reset the goals.
- Incorporating the points from Exercise 4.2 into group or organizational goal setting.

Tip 4.6

If there is a significant external change in circumstances, such as a new government policy, or a major economic or political event, revisit and adjust the goal if appropriate. If a SMARTER goal no longer becomes "achievable," then be flexible (Chapter 3) and alter your target. If a pilot plans to land at Paris and there's a thick fog there, they'll change course to land at Lyon.

Even if you or your organization is well used to the traditional SMART process and you automatically set goals accordingly, you will be able to improve using SMARTER goals.

Exercise 4.3

(approx. 20–45 minutes)

Revisit the goal(s) you set in Exercise 4.1. Apply the SMARTER goal-setting process and adjust the goal if appropriate. Consider whether the goal is an outcome, performance, or process goal. If it is a process goal, what would be a relevant performance and outcome goal?

Part II

Verbal and Non-Verbal Communication

Part II provides you with some skills that form the basis of effective communication, which will help you get the most from the topics in the rest of this book.

Chapter 5 describes how to hone your observational skills and build trust and rapport quickly.

Chapter 6 looks at how you can alter the way in which you communicate to suit the preferences of listeners.

Chapter 7 covers several essential aspects and models of language to help you influence and gain information quickly and effectively.

Building Relationships at Work

How to get people on your side

One of the Principles for Success is the ability to build and maintain good working relationships with colleagues, customers, and other stakeholders. In NLP, this is called rapport; it is fundamental to all communications and can be defined as "a feeling of trust and co-operation between people." In order to be able to build rapport, it is important that we are aware of how other people are responding. In NLP, there is a concept called sensory acuity—in other words, using your senses to watch, listen to, and in some cases, feel the subtle (sometimes extremely subtle) non-verbal signals that people are automatically sending (influenced by how they think and feel (see the left-hand side of the Communication Model diagram in Chapter 2) so that you can gain an understanding of how they are feeling and responding at any given moment. This sensory awareness is a prerequisite for rapport and we will briefly cover it before moving onto rapport.

Sensory acuity

Sensory acuity is the second of the Principles for Success (Chapter 3). It relates to taking feedback about how a conversation or communication is going and can help you communicate even more effectively in the workplace.

To illustrate this, we need to go back in time briefly. In the Introduction, I mentioned that NLP was initially developed in the 1970s by John Grinder and Richard Bandler modeling excellent communicators. One of these excellent communicators was the eminent doctor and hypnotherapist Milton Erickson. Erickson has such exquisite sensory acuity that, so the story goes, he was able to tell that a patient was going into a trance because he could see the pulse in their ankle slowing down.

You may be wondering at this point, "What has hypnosis got to do with business?" Put simply, hypnotherapists are in the business of influencing via their verbal and non-verbal communication; in the workplace, *everyone* wants to influence other people, whether it be:

- Sales people influencing customers to explain their needs so that they can better serve the customer and (hopefully) sell to them.
- Managers influencing staff to perform better.
- Staff influencing managers for a pay raise or promotion.
- Doctors influencing patients to take their medication.
- Teachers and trainers influencing students and course delegates to learn.

If you can use your sensory acuity to assess how people are feeling at any given moment (i.e. their state, as referred to in the Communication Model in Chapter 2), you are more likely to be able to proceed at the right speed and influence them, just as a hypnotherapist is better able to proceed at the right speed to induce a trance in a client who wants to stop smoking. Using some of the workplace examples above, is the customer ready to make a decision to buy or do they need more information? Have the course delegates understood or do they need more explanation?

Overall, sensory acuity helps you gain a greater understanding of how someone is feeling at any moment and hence helps you choose how and what to communicate.

Some principles of sensory acuity

Almost every person uses their sensory acuity automatically. Most people will know if their spouse, friends, or close work colleagues are in a particularly good or bad mood simply by looking at them when they walk into the room or from hearing them say "hello."

The way people do this is by comparing how someone appears now to how they normally do, or by recognizing certain subtle non-verbal signals the person is currently exhibiting and comparing this occasion with the previous times they displayed these signals (this is known in NLP as "calibrating").

What to pay attention to

Without necessarily realizing it, you will have been noticing some or all of the following non-verbal signals when recognizing how people you know well are feeling, for example:

- Breathing patterns (fast or slow, chest or abdomen).
- Pupil size (dilated or constricted).
- Eye focus.
- Fullness of the lower lip.
- Skin color change (blushing, for example).
- Clusters of gestures (such as hand movements, foot tapping, body posture).
- Voice tonality (volume, pitch, speed, intonation).
- Facial muscle and eye movements.

You can use sensory acuity with people whom you do not know well. For example, when meeting a new supplier and casually chatting before the meeting starts, pay attention to the non-verbal signals when they talk about, for example, the holiday they liked, the frustration they felt in a traffic jam, and other experiences that link to their feeling a particular way. You will be able to use this to recognize if they are feeling these states later in the conversation.

Caveats

It is important to realize that people are different from each other, and the signals that one person sends when feeling, for example, confused, may be the same as someone else feeling, for example, curious. Remember also that some people are more demonstrative than others and be wary of labeling someone's response purely by one aspect of their body language.

Story 5.1

When teaching sensory acuity in training courses, I ask people what does someone having folded arms mean. The typical reply is "they're defensive or angry." Though this may be the case, I point out that the person may be cold, they may be comfortable with her arms folded, she may have a stain on her shirt, or she may be perspiring more than usual and not want you to see it!

Please use common sense here: if someone is shouting in an abusive way, the signs about how they are feeling are evident.

In his best-selling book, *What Every BODY is Saying*, the author and former FBI investigator, Joe Navarro (whose job included identifying when people were lying), emphasizes that each person is different, and though there may be certain signs that strongly indicate how someone is feeling, he would look for patterns; for example, people demonstrating the same response in more than one situation. So, using the arm-folding example in Story 5.1, if someone folded their arms and then displayed angry behavior, be wary of the next time they fold their arms.

Tip 5.1

Though sensory acuity alone would rarely be sufficient to identify whether a client, interviewee, or colleague is not being truthful, using your sensory acuity could indicate when it might be useful to probe for more information.

Applications of sensory acuity at work

Here are some examples of how you could use sensory acuity in the workplace.

Sales:

- Identifying whether the client is ready to agree to buy or needs further information before deciding.
- Gaining credibility by being able to ask probing questions if the customer shows signs of uncertainty.

Story 5.2

One of my new students, Peter, had a meeting with a chief executive officer (CEO) and his human-resources director (HRD). The CEO was a very domineering character. At one point he said to the HRD, "I know you're happy with the level of staff engagement, aren't you?" and she replied, "Yes." But Peter had seen her agree with statements made previously (i.e. he had calibrated her "yes" signals) and this was not a true "yes." After the CEO left, Peter asked her about his question; initially she was taken aback that he had spotted it, but she then confided that she was having difficulties with the CEO and the area of staff engagement. Peter was able to work with her to begin to address this.

Appraisals:

- Is the member of staff in agreement with your comments?
- Calibrating how committed the employee is to achieving the goals.
- How truthful is your boss being about why you did not get promoted?

Interviews:

- Is the interviewee exaggerating their experience?

- Calibrating whether the example you are using to demonstrate your experience is sufficient for the interviewer.

Presentations/meetings:

- Calibrating whether your message is going down well or whether you need to adjust your approach.

Your sensory acuity skills are the foundation of the next topic: build rapport.

Rapport

Rapport is the feeling of trust and co-operation between two or more people, so that they will be more receptive to what you are saying to them. It is an essential part of building good working relationships. Bandler and Grinder noticed that Erickson, as well as having excellent sensory acuity, was able to build a deep-level rapport as a way of influencing his clients to go into a trance.

Why is rapport so useful?

Rapport is one of the Principles for Success (Chapter 3) and is fundamental to all effective communication in the workplace. You will be far more likely to be positively influenced by someone you trust and feel comfortable with than by someone you don't. Equally, you will be much better able to influence customers and colleagues if they trust you and feel comfortable with you.

Here are some specific examples of how rapport will help you at work:

- Selling, whether in the traditional sense of products and services, or selling ideas to colleagues, suppliers, patients, students.
- Being selected at interviews.
- Negotiating more effectively, including if the negotiations become tense.
- Coaching, because at times a coach will need to really challenge a client.
- Presenting ideas to groups (e.g. meetings, presentations).
- Handling conflicts and challenging conversations.

Many people I speak to have been taught about building rapport during various management and influencing-skills courses. This indicates how useful this topic is in the workplace.

Some principles underpinning rapport

There are some key principles underpinning rapport. Firstly, rapport is about influencing people appropriately, not manipulating them to do something they do not want to do. Even if the latter were possible, most businesses espouse ethical business practices, creating customer loyalty, reputation, and relationships, and generally creating "win–win" scenarios. Another principle relates to the notion that people tend to like people who are like them to some degree. (See Chapter 36 in Leigh Thompson's *The Truth about Negotiations*.)

A third principle is that most communication is non-verbal. Research by Mehrabian, Birdwhistell, and others suggests that words make up only 7 percent of communication, with voice tonality making up 38 percent and body language 55 percent. Most of our conscious attention in a conversation is taken up by listening to the words, so up to 93 percent of a communication may be outside our conscious awareness. Even if these numbers are not totally correct, we know they have some validity; if you imagine a client saying how pleased they are to see you, but in a monotonous voice, with slouched posture, and looking away from you, you would probably think that they weren't so pleased!

Research into "mirror neurons" and mother–child communication has shown that when there is rapport between two people, there is a form of "unconscious" communication, where both parties naturally feel comfortable.

Finally, rapport is something that almost everyone experiences automatically with people they like and feel comfortable with. Observe people at a business-networking event, or at a conference, and you will see people engrossed in a conversation demonstrating the signs of rapport that we will discuss in the following section.

How to build rapport

Given that most communication is non-verbal, and that people who are in some way like each other tend to like each other, if you can demonstrate non-verbally that you are like your work contacts they will probably like you, or at least feel comfortable with you.

The way to do this is by "matching" and/or "mirroring" elements of the other person's (or persons') physiology, voice tonality, or words. Matching and mirroring are similar to each other, the difference being that, in terms of physiology, if your colleague has their right hand on their chin, you would be matching them if you are facing them with your right hand on your chin, and mirroring them if you had your left hand on your chin. It is generally considered by NLP Practitioners that mirroring is more effective than matching, although I am unaware of any definitive evidence. You can also match one person's physiology with a different part of your own, for example, if they are tapping their foot, you could tap your finger at the same speed (known as "cross-over matching"). I will use the term "matching" from now onward to cover all three types.

Here are the key things you can match:

Physiology (55 percent):

- Posture (such as hand on chin, leaning forward, back, or to the side).
- Gestures (please only do this when it is *your* turn to talk).
- Breathing patterns such as speed and location (e.g. chest, stomach).
- Facial expressions.
- Amount of eye contact (though this is not traditionally covered in NLP courses, it is, nonetheless, implicit in building rapport).
- Style of dress (again, this is not a specific NLP point, although in a business context it is usually important to dress in keeping with the culture).

Voice (38 percent):

- Speed of speaking.
- Volume of speaking.
- Tone (high or low pitch, intonation).
- Timbre (the quality or resonance of the voice).

Words (7 percent):

- Amount of detail (lots of detail, just the overview, or a combination); generally, the more senior or experienced in a role someone is, the less they will require detail.

- Common experiences (for example, hobbies, holiday locations, children).

- Key words and phrases that they use or that are used in their industry/profession.

- "Predicates." These are words denoting whether the person is thinking in pictures, sounds, or feelings. For example, if someone says, "from my point of view," this indicates they are thinking in pictures (view); if they say, "that idea resonates with me," they are probably thinking in sounds (resonate). This topic is covered in detail in Chapter 6.

More specifically, you would "pace" the person by matching one or two aspects of the above until you felt there was some rapport, and then if appropriate, you would "lead" them toward where you wanted them to be. (You may hear people who have studied NLP refer to building rapport as "pacing and leading.") See "Indicators of rapport" for more on this.

It is important to remember to use common sense, and that a little goes a long way. Please do *not* match every single movement, because it will be very obvious and the other person will probably become uncomfortable. It is more effective to pick one or two elements and do it subtly, out of the other person's conscious awareness. If someone you are seeking to build rapport with happens to use exaggerated gestures or postures, you could match this to some degree, if matching it to the same degree would feel too unnatural or inappropriate (a little goes a long way).

Indicators of rapport

How would you know you were in rapport? You might observe slight skin-color changes in the other person (using your sensory acuity skills), and/or you might feel really comfortable with them, even feeling as if you've met them before or known them for a while. You might also casually touch, for example, your cheek, and if they automatically touch theirs, it indicates that you have "led" them because you are in rapport. Other ways of pacing and leading include initially altering your voice speed or volume toward the other person's level (pacing), and then once you feel you are in rapport, you would lead them to a voice speed or volume that felt more comfortable. For example, if your client naturally speaks very quickly and you naturally speak more slowly, you could increase your speed for a little while until you felt there was some rapport and then slow it down somewhat to a level that you both feel comfortable with.

Exercise 5.1

Pay attention to people in meetings or at business-networking events. Notice how they naturally match each other when they are engrossed in conversation, and how they "mismatch" when they are not enjoying the conversation and want to leave or move on to the next person.

Applications at work: Pacing and leading individuals

By now you will have realized that building rapport is so important that it underpins every working relationship, ranging from colleagues, suppliers, clients/customers, patients, students, and at meetings such as appraisals, interviews, and presentations.

The principles of pacing and leading can be applied more generally rather than simply matching body language, voice, and words. For example, if you want to persuade a colleague about an idea you have been working on, as well as building rapport as outlined above, you could pace their current level of knowledge by explaining it to them in ways that you know they would understand and gradually take them to the level of understanding that you have built up. Equally, if you know that they are the type of person who wants the information quickly, avoid wasting time with explanation unless they request it.

"Breaking" rapport can occasionally be useful too. For example, beginning to gather your papers signals that you would like the meeting to end. Or, as a salesman, leaving the client some time to reflect before actually committing to buy while you request to make a phone call or go to the restroom. This can be useful where there is a "cooling-off period," for example, on certain personal finance contracts. It is possible that you might have built such a high degree of rapport that the client will buy from you, only to reflect and cancel due to "buyer's remorse." It is far better to gently and briefly break rapport by, for example, going to the restroom, in order to give the client time to reflect alone before signing the forms.

Applications at work: Pacing and leading groups

You can build rapport with groups as well as with individuals. Here are some examples.

When doing a presentation to a group, at or near the start, you can ask for a show of hands on both sides of a particular topic and raise your hand as you ask it. For example, I will often ask, "Who has heard me speak before?" followed by "And who is seeing me for the first time?" By doing this, you are in rapport with the group, because almost all (if not all) of the audience will have raised their hand to match/mirror yours. Another question I have found to be useful is "Raise your hand if you'd like to finish a little early today?" (I rarely need to ask the opposite question!)

If you are at a meeting or doing a presentation where you know there will be some resistance to people being there, for example, a compulsory meeting at 4 p.m. on a Friday before a holiday weekend, rather than being really energetic from the start, you could indicate that you are aware of how they are feeling and "pace" it before "leading." For example, you can say, "I know it's four o' clock on Friday afternoon before a long weekend, and I guess some of you may not be looking forward to this meeting." (Pause and look for signs of agreement.) "So here's what I suggest: let's be really focused on getting the meeting done as quickly and productively as possible so that we can all go home and enjoy the weekend." Please reflect before you do this to be as sure as you can be that your assumption is correct; if they were looking forward to the meeting, you would have inadvertently planted negative thoughts in their minds!

If you are at a meeting with a group of prospective clients, or at a panel interview, you will find that there will be some common postures (for example, some might have their legs crossed, others their hand on their chin, others leaning forward, others leaning back). Pick a leg-related posture and an arm-related posture that match as many people as possible. When you feel that you have built rapport with those people (probably after a minute or two), subtly change so that you are matching the others that you have not matched, and keep doing this so that you are in rapport with everyone for large portions of the meeting. If there happens to be someone who appears most influential (not necessarily the most senior), concentrate on maintaining rapport with that person throughout, in addition to periodically switching to build rapport with everyone else.

Breaking rapport with a group might be useful. As a manager, you can leave the room during a team meeting, leaving your team to make some decisions that they will be responsible for implementing before returning to the room.

Communicating in Everyone's Language

Altering your style to suit the listener

If you talk to a man in a language he understands, that goes to his head. If you talk to him in his language, that goes to his heart.
—Nelson Mandela

In English, as in many other languages, there are four main preferences that influence the type of language that a person will use. Knowing about this will help you to put your point across in such a way that everyone will grasp what you are saying and therefore see what you mean, because you will be communicating in the way they automatically process information, even if they are not consciously aware of it.

Why is this so useful?

There are several reasons why this material is so useful at work, both for individuals and groups. You will be able to:

- Improve your communication when selling, presenting, managing, advertising, and negotiating, because you will be able to communicate in the way other people think and want to receive information. This helps to avoid situations where you say the same thing to different people and get very different responses.
- Improve your capabilities where they are linked to senses, such as listening skills, creativity, and creative problem solving.
- Coach others in the above areas.
- Build rapport using words.

Before we expand on this, we need to cover some fundamentals.

How we gather and process information

As you remember from the Communication Model (Chapter 2), we receive external information using our five senses and process the information internally using these same five senses. Additionally, we have an internal dialogue about this information (i.e. putting words to it). These senses are known as "representational systems," that is, how we represent (or *re-present* to ourselves) information. Our representational systems are:

- See (visual).
- Hear (auditory).
- Feel (kinesthetic).
- Smell (olfactory).
- Taste (gustatory).

In addition to these five senses, there is an internal dialogue about events. This internal dialogue (or self-talk) is known as "auditory digital." For example, you may just have been promoted and become entitled to a company car. When you go into the showroom, you might see (visual) a particular car and you might say to yourself (auditory digital), "That's the one I want."

Though each of us uses all of the representational systems to some degree, many people have one or two senses that they prefer to use (known as their "preferred" or "primary" representational system). We will cover preferred systems in the next section. Generally in Western culture, the olfactory and gustatory systems, though important for survival, are not as important as they are for people living a more subsistence type of lifestyle, so the other three senses, together with auditory digital, are more dominant. Let's look at these four main representational systems.

- **Visual:** this consists of external images, creating images, and visualizing in our mind, as well as remembering pictures/images you have seen.
- **Auditory:** this consists of external sounds, creating sounds in our mind, and remembering sounds/music/words you have heard.

- **Kinesthetic:** this is made up of external touch, internal sensations, and emotions, as well as bodily awareness.
- **Auditory digital:** this is your internal dialogue and assessment about a topic.

Preferred representational systems

In the field of NLP it is generally thought that approximately:

- 35–40 percent of people prefer the visual system.
- 20–25 percent prefer the auditory or auditory digital system.
- 40 percent of people prefer the kinesthetic system.

This is important to know because, as a generalization, you tend to communicate according to *your* preferences, which can be effective provided that you are communicating with people who have a similar preference, and not so effective if they have a different preference from you.

Certain professions may have a stronger bias toward a specific system because of the inherent nature of the work:

- Architects and designers tend to prefer the visual system.
- Musicians and telesales people tend to prefer the auditory system.
- Computer engineers (doing repairs) and physiotherapists tend to prefer the kinesthetic system.
- Accountants, lawyers, and business analysts tend to prefer the auditory digital system.

Exercise 6.1

(approx. 10 minutes)

Please complete the preferred representational system questionnaire. This will indicate your preferred system.

Representational System Preference Questionnaire

Step 1: For each of the following statements, please place a number next to every phrase. Use the following system to indicate your preferences:

4 = Most accurately describes your preference.

3 = Next best description of your preference.

2 = Next best after 3 above of your preference.

1 = Least likely description of your preference.

At this point, ignore the reference to a, b, c, and d. You will be using this information in step 2. Please note that the order of a, b, c, and d changes for each question.

1. Generally I make important decisions based on:

   a. ___ Which way looks best to me.

   b. ___ Which way sounds best to me.

   c. ___ Review, analysis, and consideration of the issues.

   d. ___ My gut feelings, what feels best to me.

2. During a heated debate, I am most likely to be influenced by:

   b. ___ People's tone of voice.

   a. ___ Whether or not I can see the other person's point of view.

   c. ___ The logic of the other person's argument.

   d. ___ How I feel about the topics.

3. During a meeting, I like information to be presented:

   a. ___ In a way that is neat and tidy, with pictures and diagrams.

   d. ___ In a way that I can grasp and that I can get a hands-on experience.

   c. ___ In a logical, rational way, so that I can understand.

   b. ___ In the form of a conversation, so that we can discuss and I can ask questions.

4. My favorite hobbies and pastimes typically involve:

   b. ___ Listening to music, the radio, or talking with people.

   a. ___ Watching films and other visual arts.

d. ___ Playing sports, doing activities, and generally moving about.

c. ___ Reading, learning, analyzing, and generally using my mind.

5. I tend to resolve problems by:

a. ___ Looking at the situation and all the alternatives, possibly using diagrams.

b. ___ Talking through the situation with friends or colleagues.

c. ___ Analyzing the situation and choosing the approach that makes most sense.

d. ___ Trusting my intuition and gut feelings.

6. When with my friends:

a. ___ I enjoy watching how they interact and behave.

d. ___ I tend to hug them, or sit close to them, when speaking to them.

c. ___ I am interested in their rationale, reasons, and ideas when talking to them.

b. ___ I enjoy talking and listening to them.

7. I prefer to learn a particular aspect of a sport or activity by:

a. ___ Watching how the teacher or coach does it.

d. ___ Having the teacher or coach adjust my body into the right position.

b. ___ Listening to explanations, discussing, and asking questions.

c. ___ Understanding the reasons and rationale for doing it in a certain way.

8. When at a presentation, I am most interested by:

c. ___ The logic and rationale of the presentation.

b. ___ The tone of voice and the way the presenter speaks.

a. ___ The visual aids used by the presenter.

d. ___ The opportunity to get to grips with the content, perhaps by actually doing an activity.

Scoring the Questionnaire

Step 2: On Table 6.1, write the scores associated with each letter, and then total each column.

Step 3: The totals give an indication of your relative preference for each of the four major representational systems (a = Visual, b = Auditory, c = Auditory Digital, d = Kinaesthetic). Remember, these scores are preferences, *not* statements about capability or about who you are as a person.

Table 6.1

	a	b	c	d
1				
2				
3				
4				
5				
6				
7				
8				
TOTAL	V=	A=	Ad=	K=

Tip 6.1

Please note that the percentages above and the results from Exercise 6.1 are indications, and "preference" does not necessarily equate to "competence." For example, if your least preferred system is auditory, it does not mean that you are a "bad listener."

Recognizing preferred representational systems

Here are some indications of how to recognize preferred representational systems in the workplace and hence how people will *tend* to behave.

This section has some generalizations that may not be true for every single person.

Visual (i.e. they prefer to think in pictures and diagrams):

- Speak fast (they think in pictures, and a picture paints a thousand words) and gesticulate quickly.

- Use "visual" language such as *see, look, appear, focus, paint a picture, mental image, clear, in view of, hazy, show, look forward to, illuminate, visualize, imagine, review, I see your point, short-sighted, take a dim view of.*

- Have hobbies and do work that involves seeing things, such as art, watching films, or photography, or they like the visual aspect of their pastimes, such as looking at scenery when walking in the country.

- Remember things better when they have seen them, and especially like diagrams, flow charts, and pictures.

- Learn by seeing, such as by looking at diagrams, videos, flow charts, and pictures.

- Like things to be neat and tidy—the way something or someone looks is important.

Auditory (i.e. they prefer to communicate using words):

- Speak at a medium pace, often in a rhythmic or melodious way.

- Use "auditory" language such as *hear, sound, listen, speak, discuss, converse, tune in/tune out, resonate, I'm all ears, voice an opinion, ask, tell, announce, rings a bell, music to my ears, loud and clear, the same wavelength, harmonize.*

- Have hobbies and do work that involves hearing or words, such as reciting poetry, listening to music, speaking to their friends on the phone, or they like the auditory aspect of their pastimes, such as hearing the sounds of nature when walking in the country.

- Remember things better when they have discussed or heard them.

- Learn by hearing, by listening to audio material, or hearing explanations.

Auditory digital (i.e. they prefer to think in ideas and to analyze):

- Want to understand how ideas work.

- Are interested in ideas that make sense and are logical.

- Use language that is not "sensory specific," such as *conceive, evaluate, assess, think, understand, know, learn, process, decide, consider, change, makes sense, logical process, modify our thinking, change of mind, the rationale is.*

- Need facts, figures, and evidence.

- Can exhibit the characteristics of any of the three other main systems.

Kinesthetic (i.e. they prefer to feel/experience things):

- Speak at a slow pace.

- Use "kinesthetic" language such as *solid, grasp, connect, concrete, make contact, kick some ideas around, hard, soft, rough, smooth the way for something, get hold of, get in touch with, catch onto, touch base with, get a handle on, lay our cards on the table, pull some strings.*

- Have hobbies and do work that involves touching or emotions, such as physiotherapy, pottery, or sports, or they like the kinesthetic aspect of their pastimes, such as feeling the fresh air when walking in the country (walking is a kinesthetic activity anyway).

- Remember things better when they have experienced them.

- Learn best by doing, by putting into practice and experimenting with what they have been taught.

By being able to recognize someone's preference, you will be more likely to be able to present information in a way that they like to receive it, and you'll also be better able to influence them.

Using representational systems at work

For yourself: Because most people communicate according to their own sensory preferences, enhancing the ease with which you can use any of the four main representational systems will help you become more flexible in communicating with people regardless of their sensory preferences.

This fluency, in addition to being able to recognize other people's preferred system, will help you communicate and build rapport, regardless of the work you do.

Tip 6.2

You can enhance your ability to access and use your less-favored representational system(s) by way of relevant practice. Here are some examples.

- Visual: memorize work-related diagrams (gradually increasing the complexity) or even do "spot the difference" puzzles.

- Auditory: listen to the radio or audio learning material.

- Kinesthetic: check how you feel about work-related issues or, if appropriate, walk through a process step by step.

- Auditory digital: think about the logical reasons and/or seek appropriate facts and figures about a work-related topic.

With other individuals and groups: When presenting information to a specific individual at work (such as a customer, staff member, supplier, trainee), where possible seek to identify their preferred system and then present information accordingly, by focusing the presentation style as follows:

- Pictures and diagrams (visual). (Make them neat!)
- Discussion (auditory).
- Involve the person in some way, for example, by letting them try out your new product (kinesthetic).
- Facts and figures (auditory digital).

Please remember to use a combination of the above, because even if the person has a preference for one system, this does *not* mean that they will not use the others to some degree.

Story 6.1

One of my colleagues used to be an educational sales representative, with around 200 head teachers and college principals in her sales area. After she completed her NLP Practitioner course, she made a note of the preferred representational system of each of her sales contacts, using the information shown in "Recognizing preferred representational systems" (page 80):

- For those with a visual preference, she wanted to see them face to face, making sure that she was always neatly dressed and that she gave them glossy brochures or showed them products.

- For those with an auditory preference, she would phone them for a chat, and whenever she saw them she made sure that she had time to chat with them about products.

- For those with a kinesthetic preference, she would take them cakes or make sure that she could have a sandwich with them (eating cakes and sandwiches is a kinesthetic as well as a gustatory activity) and she would give them the chance to try out the products.

- For those with an auditory digital preference, she would make sure that she knew the relevant facts, figures, and scientific studies.

Within six months she had significantly improved her sales performance.

Exercise 6.2

Following on from Story 6.1, identify the one or two pre-ferred representational systems of important work colleagues and clients and present information to them accordingly.

Following on from an earlier point, use a combination of all four presentation methods when presenting information to groups. This will help engage the whole audience in the topic. The same principles can be used when presenting ideas by way of e-mail or reports. When making "formal" presentations or running training courses, consider using neat and colorful flip charts instead of (or in addition to) PowerPoint slides. The flip charts can then be put on the wall to create a visual reminder throughout the course, as opposed to a PowerPoint slide that disappears as you move on to the next slide.

Tip 6.3

If you manage a team, ask them all to complete the representational system preference questionnaire, and then discuss the results and how it reflects their individual preferences for receiving information.

Another use of representational systems is in the area of consultancy and problem solving. This is best illustrated by the following example.

Story 6.2

An ex-colleague told me how he used the principles of representational systems to help a client make more progress in two hours than a major consultancy firm was able to do in several weeks. He and I spoke at an NLP conference and we decided to demonstrate how the process worked. There were 13 attendees, none of whom had met each other before. One was a manager of a steel factory that had some production problems; no one else knew anything about steel production. Under the guidance of the factory manager, the other 12 delegates laid out pieces of paper on the floor to represent the different departments and areas involved in the process. This provided a **visual** image of the situation. There were various discussions about the current and desired situation, including relevant facts, which allowed for **auditory** and **auditory digital** processing. A small object was used to represent the movement of steel through the factory and delegates were encouraged to move the object and write notes if they wanted to. This was the **kinaesthetic** element.

Within the 45 minutes allotted, the factory manager said that he had at least two excellent ideas directly as a result of this "consultancy" project from complete novices.

Sensory-based language

Talk to people in their own language. If you do it well, they'll say, "God, he said exactly what I was thinking." And when they begin to respect you, they'll follow you to the death.

—Lee Iacocca, former president at Ford Motor Company and Chrysler

We can extend the use of representational systems to the area of language. As we covered in Chapter 2, language is the way that we turn our thoughts into words. Given that we think in pictures, sounds, feelings, and self-talk, it is not surprising that our words reflect this. Earlier in the chapter, we looked at how to recognize someone's preferred representational system; one of the indicators was the words they use. For example, someone thinking visually will use words and phrases such as *look, see, watch, paint a picture, focus,* and *point of view.* By being able to tune in to what people are saying, you will be able to quickly pick up and understand how they are thinking. In NLP, words and phrases indicating which representational system someone is using are called "predicates."

Why are predicates so useful?

Being able to use appropriate predicates is one of the ways you can use words to build rapport (see page 63). This is because it helps you to communicate in a way that is being used to process at that moment by your client, colleague, interviewer, and so on.

Linked to this, given that we think using our senses, using sensory-based words will engage people at work more than using more neutral words. This is particularly useful for advertising, as many adverts seek to activate our senses. For example, newspaper adverts often use glossy images and radio adverts use catchy jingles.

Using predicates

Under the section, "Recognizing preferred representational systems" (page 80), I listed several predicates for each of the four systems. These are examples, and not an exhaustive list. Unless you are writing to someone whose representational system preference you know *and* where you know only that person will be reading the information, I suggest that you use a combination of predicates appropriately when writing e-mails, sales letters, advertising copy, and reports (even if reports are very factual, using predicates will engage the reader), when making presentations and the other examples covered under "Using representational systems at work."

Exercise 6.3

Review your e-mails, your company's advertising and publicity (including Websites) to check that predicates from all four senses have been used sufficiently. Be aware of your own preferences, so that you use an appropriate mix of all four groups of predicates.

As you read the remainder of this book or revisit earlier sections, notice how many times I use predicates and that I use all four types.

Tip 6.4

Practice developing fluency with predicates relating to your least preferred system(s), so that you can more easily see eye to eye with colleagues, be on their wavelength, really connect with and understand them!

Before we leave the subject of representational systems and predicates, there is one other relevant topic, known as "eye patterns."

Eye patterns

One other indicator of how someone is thinking is the direction in which their eyes look. Based on some research and simple observation, the direction of someone's eye movements indicates which representational system they are accessing at any given moment. Diagram 6.1 shows the eye patterns for the vast majority of people, shown as you look at them.

- Vc is visual construct, that is, creating a picture of something you haven't seen.
- Vr is visual remembered, that is, remembering a picture of something you have seen.
- Ac is auditory construct, that is, creating a sound of something or words you haven't heard.
- Ar is auditory remembered, that is, remembering a sound of something or of words you have heard.
- Ad is auditory digital, that is, talking to yourself, or saying something in your own voice.
- K is kinesthetic, that is, getting in touch with feelings.

Diagram 6.1

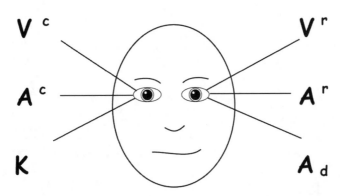

If you see someone's eyes go to a particular quadrant when thinking about a question or when speaking, it is an indication that they are accessing that particular representational system. If so, use the relevant predicates when speaking to them. For example, if you see someone's eyes go to the kinesthetic quadrant, you could say, "How does that feel?" or "How do you feel about that?"

Please use common sense with this. Someone looking up might not be accessing visual; they might simply have seen a fly on the wall. In my experience, some NLP students place too much emphasis on eye patterns. This indicator can provide useful information but it is not definitive evidence of how someone is thinking.

There are some NLP professionals who have found that a relatively small percentage of people can be "reverse-organized" (often lefthanders), whereby the items shown on the right-hand side are on the left-hand side and vice versa. You could identify whether someone is reverse-organized by paying attention to where their eyes go when they are speaking and thinking.

7

The Power of Language

Advanced speaking and listening skills at work

Change your language and you change your thoughts.
—Karl Albrecht, billionaire co-founder of the Aldi supermarket chain

In the previous chapter, we discussed some aspects of language and how to use these at work. In this chapter, we will cover how to use other aspects of language to enhance your ability to communicate to colleagues, customers, and other stakeholders. In particular, we will look at how to:

- Think in terms of the big picture or detail as appropriate, and to change the "level" of the communication.
- Use language to encourage lateral thinking and brainstorming.
- Understand the power of some everyday words.
- Use language that is deliberately vague to influence at work.
- Ask insightful and relevant questions.
- Use stories and analogies effectively at work.

Please note that though there is some terminology and names of language patterns used in this chapter, it is not a chapter on grammar. In this chapter, I will highlight how the language patterns and models which you will learn here are used in *every* verbal communication at work. The only question is how effectively are they used?

Why are we covering language?

As we have already seen, language is one of the key filters in the Communication Model and words are important when maintaining rapport, especially once rapport has initially been built. Effective use of language can also help with almost all business activities involving presenting ideas and asking questions, such as:

- Selling, marketing, and advertising.
- Influencing staff, colleagues, patients, and suppliers.
- Negotiations.
- Consultancy.
- Coaching.
- Training and teaching.
- Presenting.
- Interviewing (as interviewer or interviewee).

Let's look at the first main topic, known as the Hierarchy of Ideas.

The Hierarchy of Ideas

This model relates to the level of detail involved in a communication, which can range from the big picture and abstract (known in NLP as *big chunk*) through to the specific and detailed (*small chunk*). We can use this model to change our own (or other people's) level from big chunk to small chunk or vice versa, and also to think laterally. Examples of abstract (big chunk) ideas in the workplace include concepts such as *efficiency, productivity, prosperity, equal opportunities,* and *growth prospects.* Detail (small chunk) is obtained by getting into the specifics of *who, what, where, when,* and *how.*

One of the main reasons why this is so useful is that, according to *Please Understand Me* by Keirsey and Bates, which explains the well-known Myers–Briggs Type Indicator (MBTI) personality-profiling system, the differences between big and small chunk are a major source of communication difficulties and disagreements between people.

Other business uses of this model include:

- Being able to build rapport at work (one of the ways to build rapport using words is to match "chunk size"). For example, if a director has a preference for big chunk, typically he would want an overview of your message rather than lots of detail.

- Improving your chances of promotion, because generally the more senior you are, the more you will need to be able to see the overview as well as being able to drill down into the detail if there are problems. For example, a finance director will need to understand how the whole business works and how the finances of the business are impacted by changes in foreign-exchange rates and the economic situation, whereas an accounts clerk is more likely to be concerned with details shown on specific invoices.

You can use the Hierarchy of Ideas to move to a bigger chunk (known as *chunking up* or *upward*) for the purpose of, for example:

- Gaining agreement and buy-in, when negotiating and speaking to teams. Most people would agree that prosperity (a big chunk concept) is desirable; they may disagree on how to get there, or what prosperity actually means.

- Setting mission statements and values (both are big chunk concepts) for an organization, which helps to create an engaged workforce.

- Agreeing on the purpose of a new policy or system so that management can select one that fully meets their needs.

Conversely, you can use the Hierarchy of Ideas to move to a smaller chunk (known as *chunking down* or *downward*) for the purpose of, for example:

- Making sure that everyone involved in a project knows exactly what they are doing and when, so that targets or deadlines are met.

- Coaching or managing people around the specific tasks required to achieve their goals.

- Investigating problems or underperformance to help resolve it.

How to use the principles of chunking

Let's assume that you are discussing the purchase of a new computer system. Here are some questions to ask if you want to chunk up.

- What is the benefit/purpose of the new system?
- What will the new system get for you/us?
- What is the new system an example of?
- What is the intention of having the new system?

As the speaker, you would choose the question(s) most relevant to the specific situation and what you wanted to gain from asking the question, given what had been said previously in the discussion.

To chunk down, you could ask the following questions.

- Who exactly will authorize the purchase of the new system? Who will we buy it from?
- When will the purchase be authorized? When will it be delivered?
- How much will the new system cost? How exactly are we going to use this new system?
- Where exactly are you going to put the new system?
- What is the specification of the new system?
- What are examples/types of new systems that we could buy in the future?

Exercise 7.1

Notice for yourself whether you are more comfortable in the big picture, the detail, or are equally comfortable with both. You can do this in several ways, for example, noticing how comfortable (or not) you are when getting into the details of a situation, asking yourself the chunking-up and chunking-down questions about various work challenges and noticing where you feel most comfortable. You can also do this with clients, colleagues, and staff by noticing how much detail they give you, and also how tolerant they are to detail. This point is expanded in Chapter 15 in the section on Chunk Size Filter.

Remember that one way to build rapport using words is to match the amount of detail that someone prefers. You can use the Hierarchy of Ideas to chunk laterally, for example, if you have reached an impasse when negotiating or in a brainstorming session. You do this as follows:

1. Ask a chunking-up question from those listed on page 97.

2. Chunk down, asking for a *different* example or a *different* way.

Story 7.1 illustrates this.

Story 7.1

One of my NLP mentors was hired to help a company negotiate with a trade union. He spoke to the company management and asked what they wanted, then chunked up a couple of levels until very abstract concepts were mentioned, such as "expansion." He spoke to the unions, and unsurprisingly they wanted a pay raise. He asked them some chunking-up questions and found that the real purpose of the pay raise was so that the employees could have a "comfortable retirement."

Thinking laterally, he asked himself, the unions, and the management how else employees could have a comfortable retirement rather than by having the level of pay increase being demanded. They realized that increased pension contributions would be an acceptable way forward and hence proceeded to agree on the various details.

So, in this example, chunking up to "comfortable retirement," and then asking for a different way to achieve this, led to an agreement.

Tip 7.1

To enhance your ability to work with both detail and abstract concepts, pick a current challenge at work and chunk up a few levels until you reach a highly abstract concept (for example, profitability, staff engagement, or fulfillment). Chunk downward a few levels from the challenge until you understand the necessary detail. If you are naturally stronger at one level, work on the opposite until you are more comfortable at that level if that would be useful to you.

The Hierarchy of Ideas can be summarized in Diagram 7.1.

Applications in the workplace

You can use the Hierarchy of Ideas in several ways at work:

- Career progression. You could frequently ask yourself chunking-up questions about work issues and topics, for example, an accounts clerk looking to advance their career might ask themself, "What's the purpose of making sure that all the invoices are dispatched correctly and on time?" Generally, the higher you go in an organisation, the more you will be expected to see a bigger picture.

- Coaching/managing other people to improve by using the relevant questions.

- Goal setting. If you review Chapter 4, you will notice that there are questions that chunk up and others that chunk down.

- Creating alternative solutions and problem solving using lateral chunking.

- Conflict resolution and negotiations. Chunk up and then chunk down only as quickly as it enables you to maintain rapport.

- Fact-finding and troubleshooting (chunking down).

- Meetings. Ensure that they stay on track by knowing the purpose of the meeting (chunking up), and also if a comment appears to be taking the meeting off track, asking (politely) how that point specifically relates to the purpose of the meeting.

- Creating a corporate vision or mission statement (by chunking up to a really abstract level).
- Generating action plans at meetings or for projects (chunking down).

Diagram 7.1

Level	Some Useful Questions	Example 1
Big chunk/abstract/ general/overview (potential areas of agreement)	↑ What is the pupose of X? What will X do for you? What is your intention by doing X? What is X an example of? **Chunking up(ward)**	Fulfilling life ↑ More money ↑ Save time, do more ↑ Faster work ↑ **Computer** ↙ ↘ Make Part ↓ ↓ Brand X CPU ↓ ↓ Model Y Processor
	Chunking down(ward) What are examples of this? Who/what/when/ where/how specifically? How do you know specifically? ↓	

Having covered the idea of chunking, let's now move on to another model of language.

Implied meanings within language

Within NLP there is a topic called "linguistic presuppositions" (these are completely different from the NLP Presuppositions covered in Chapter 3). Linguistic presuppositions can be defined as what is automatically assumed in a sentence or phrase in order for that sentence to make sense. For example, the sentence "The man sees the dog" presupposes three things:

- There is a man.
- He can see.
- There is a dog.

Though this example is very obvious, this model of language will help you to refine your communication so that you influence the listener(s) and readers the way you want to, and to better understand how people think by how they speak (remember Covey's quote (page 38): "Seek first to understand, then be understood").

Moreover, if you read the editorial articles in a quality national newspaper you will find several examples of how the editor uses linguistic presuppositions (whether they are aware of it or not). You cannot avoid using these models because they are inherent in language; you can, however, choose to learn how to use them even more effectively than you currently do.

The main forms of linguistic presupposition

We will cover 10 main forms. I will give you the name and brief explanation of the presupposition with an example of how you can use each of them in the workplace. There are almost unlimited uses of this type of language, so there will be no specific section on application in the workplace. For more extensive coverage and a list of 29 types of linguistic presupposition, please read *The Structure of Magic, Volume I* by Richard Bandler and John Grinder.

The statements that follow are stand-alone statements purely to illustrate the points being made. It is important to remember that these sentences do not have to be *true*; they do need to be *plausible* given the context in which they are said. In each of the examples that follow, the presupposition being demonstrated is in bold for your reference.

As with all topics covered in this book, please ensure that you are in rapport, have a positive intention for the other person(s), and use common sense when using these language patterns.

Existence

These are nouns, places and people, and every sentence will have at least one presupposition of existence included in it. When managing a member of staff, you could say, "Let me know when you've found **the solution**," or "You haven't found **the solution** yet"; both presuppose that a solution exists, which can motivate your colleague to keep searching for one.

Necessity

These are verbs such as *have to, got to, should, must,* and *need to,* which indicate the rules or beliefs that someone has. You can use these verbs if you want to create some form of rule or strongly encourage people to do something.

- "We **need to** hurry up."
- "We **should** be hitting our targets this year."
- "You've **got to** get this right."

Possibility/Impossibility

These are verbs that imply that things are possible or not possible, such as *can/can't, could/couldn't, might/might not, is possible/isn't possible.*

- "We **can't** tell our boss this."
- "We **could** exceed our targets."
- "You **can** do a great presentation."

You can use these when advertising to create the impression that something will become possible for the customer once they have purchased your product/service (notice the second word in this sentence: this is another example of how this linguistic presupposition can be used).

Causation

These are words or verbs that imply some form of causation or link, for example, *if...then, because, make, cause, as you...then you.* You can use these types of words to create a linkage in someone's mind, if that would be useful.

- "**Because** you've made so many cold calls this quarter, you'll become more successful."
- "**If** you present well, (**then**) you'll be noticed."
- "Learning from mistakes **makes** you more effective."

Equivalences

These are when two things or concepts are made to appear equal or synonymous, for example, verbs such as *to be, to mean, to represent.*

- "You **are** a good negotiator" (i.e. "you" equals "good negotiator").
- "Keeping eye contact when interviewing **means** you are interested."
- "My boss shouting **means** she is really passionate about results."
- "$1,000 **represents** good value."

You can use these to create a relationship or connection between two concepts (e.g. "you" and "good negotiator," "$1,000" and "good value"). Please note that "causation" relates to a sequence, whereas "equivalence" relates to things being simultaneous.

Awareness

This presupposition relates to people being able to be aware of something and is indicated by the use of words relating to senses or awareness, for example, *see, hear, feel, understand, realize, notice,* and *to be aware of.* You can use these types of presuppositions to reduce the likelihood of objections or doubt about whether something exists.

- "John **saw** the gap in the market" (the reader/listener would probably not question whether there was in fact a gap in the market).
- "You **realized** that there was a great opportunity."
- "She **noticed** the excellent atmosphere in the office."

It is also interesting that the above sentences could be stated in the negative, where the presuppositions would still apply. So, "John didn't **see** the gap in the market" still presupposes that there's a gap in the market.

Time

The concept of time is really important in how we create our reality. Though some of the finer details are outside the scope of this book, even the following simple example will illustrate the impact.

- "We have a problem" (action is probably required).
- "We had a problem" (no action is required).

Presuppositions of time can be indicated by words such as *before*, *after*, *then*, *now*, *stop*, *yet*, and by changing the verb's tense.

- "Please let me know your plans **after** you've made your decision."
- "**Before** you leave the office today, please check that the presentation is finished."
- Staff member: "I've been having a problem with Joe." Coach/ Manager: "Okay, what **has been** the problem?" This subtly puts the problem into the past, rather than "Okay, what is the problem?" which unfortunately keeps it alive for the staff member.

Adjective/Adverb

Adjectives (which describe nouns) and adverbs (which describe verbs, and usually end in "-ly") can add impact to a sentence.

- "I'm wondering how **easily** you'll be able to find the solution" ("easily" focuses attention on how easy it will be rather than whether a solution exists).
- "How **quickly** will you be able to get me the report?" (presupposes that the person will be able to do it).
- Client: "This situation has been causing us delays for a while." Consultant (wanting to reassure the client that they are experts and can fix the problem): "Because we've been in this industry for years, we've seen relatively **simple** problems like this before. We can easily have it sorted for you in a week."

Or

Or indicates that there is a choice. Sometimes in business you want to reduce the possibly endless choices, for example:

- "We can meet on Friday at 3:15 **or** Tuesday at 2:00. Which would you prefer?"
- "Cash **or** credit card?"

Ordinal/numerical

This relates to sequences or numbers of events, such as *first, last, next, second, initial,* and *final.*

- "My **latest** book is about selling" (presupposes that the person has written books previously). Similarly, "My **fourth** book" implies that there have been three previous books, and possibly subsequent books.
- "Here's the fifth and **final** point."
- "Once you've done that, let me know and I'll give you the next installment of the story" (presupposes that there is something else to be learned or done).

Putting it all together

Scenario: a director addressing their team at the start of the annual staff meeting.

Good morning. Welcome to our third annual staff meeting. And the fact that there is such a big turnout means that you're all extremely excited to take the organization forward to the next level. The main reason we're all here is so that we can look for even better ways to do this after last year's great improvement. And we have to move forward because standing still means falling behind our competitors. And whether we move forward quickly or slightly less quickly, our aim has to be focused on our success and on becoming number one.

Exercise 7.2

(approx. 5 minutes)

Read through the above paragraph and see if you can spot how many examples of linguistic presuppositions are used. (Check your answers against those in Appendix A.)

Small words with big meanings

Following on from the previous topic, here are some small words that have disproportionately large meanings, which are often outside the conscious awareness of the speaker or listener.

Small word: *But (although, however)*

Implied Meaning: *But* negates what has previously been said, (as do the other two words to a lesser extent). "That was a great presentation, *but* (*however, although*) you could make it even better by..." implies that it *wasn't* a great presentation.

Comment: It is much more useful to use *and* instead of *but*, unless you **do** want to negate what has been said. (For example, if the speaker mentions something negative such as all the difficulties they have had meeting the deadline, you can reply, "Yes, it was difficult, but you've learned so much from it.")

Small word: *Try*

Implied Meaning: *Try* implies that something will be difficult, and/or you might not succeed. As a manager, do you want your staff member to *try* to get you the report at 5 p.m. today, or to get you the report at 5 p.m. today?

Comment: Remove the word *try* from your vocabulary, unless it is in a situation where the person has little competence in the area and you want them to experiment/try something new.

Small word: *Don't*

Implied Meaning: If you ask someone *not* to do something, they have to think about doing it (even momentarily) before they can think of an alternative (don't think about your happiest moment now). This is particularly relevant when the subject relates to an automatic (unconscious) response, such as, "Don't worry," or "Don't analyze my motives."

Comment: Tell someone what you want them to do rather than what you don't want them to do. If it is important to say what you don't want them to do, emphasize what you do want them to do: "Relax," or "Go with the flow."

Small word: *Or*

Implied Meaning: As we know from the previous section, *or* can sometimes limit the perception someone has about their range of options. On my training courses, when I say, "You can do X or Y" and ask them how many options they have, the usual reply is, "one" or "two." In practice, there are numerous options if you include all the other options that could exist apart from X or Y.

Comment: Whenever you hear the word *or*, and you do not want your or other people's thinking to be limited (for example in brainstorming meetings), mention that it could be useful to explore other options apart from those that are presented.

Small word: *Yet*

Implied Meaning: Adding *yet* to the end of a sentence can change the meaning significantly. "I can't do presentations" is very different than "I can't do presentations yet."

Comment: Adding *yet* when someone states an apparent limitation can open the door of possibility.

Small word: *If, when*

Implied Meaning: *If* implies conditionality; *when* implies that it will happen.

Comment: Choose which will be most useful in the situation: "If the Board rejects our proposal..." or "When you buy this product...."

Small word: *Can, Can't*

Implied Meaning: The word *can* and its negative *can't*, have two possible meanings. One meaning is that the person is not allowed or authorized to do something; the other meaning is that the person does not have the capability to do something.

Comment: Sometimes it can be useful to seek clarification about what someone means if they say they *can't* do something, or to clarify what you mean when you use *can* or *can't*.

Small word: *Is*

Implied Meaning: As we have seen before, the verb *to be* indicates that something equals something else. Unfortunately the word *is* is sometimes misused, for example, "This is difficult to do," or "It is hard to do X." The word *is* gives the sentence the same construction and validity as "The sun is hot."

Comment: It is more useful for the speaker to say instead, "I haven't (yet) found it easy to do X." This language helps the speaker to "own" the specific challenge, rather than using language which could create the impression that it absolutely **is** a particular way.

Exercise 7.3

Pay attention to what people are saying at meetings and notice how they use the small words above, and what impact these words have on you and on the people around you. In your mind, decide what you would say to make the message even more effective. As a separate exercise, practice using these words (or one of the relevant alternatives suggested above) to enhance the message you wish to send.

Abstract language

Returning to the Hierarchy of Ideas and the notion of abstract and specific thinking, there are two language models that can be extremely useful in the workplace. The first uses abstract language and is based on the language patterns used by the eminent hypnotherapist, Milton Erickson. He used language in such a way that it appeared vague and abstract, which enabled his clients to make up their own meaning in their head. He found it to be an excellent way to bypass "resistance" that clients might have against going into a trance. Unsurprisingly, his language model is known as the Milton Model.

Why learn about abstract language?

These language patterns are extremely useful for influencing people and, indeed, there is an excellent book called *Unlimited Selling Power* by the leading business sales consultants, Dr. Donald J. Moine and Dr. Kenneth Lloyd, which explains how to use these hypnotic language patterns in the world of sales. They can also be used in a variety of situations where you want to influence, for example, in presentations and meetings. Because these language patterns are used every day at work, learning how to use them effectively will help you to influence more effectively.

Story 7.2

One of my fellow NLP Trainers said that she noticed that all businesses used these language patterns daily, because they are part of everyday language. The problem was that these patterns were used in an ineffective way, which often caused the opposite effect to that which was intended. (By the way, there are at least five examples of abstract language patterns in this story, which you will be able to spot once you have read this section.)

There are around 22 abstract language patterns, and I will list and briefly explain the 15 most relevant to the workplace, with examples, with the subsequent two sections giving guidance on how to use them at work. Some of the patterns have already been covered in the section on linguistic presuppositions. The name of the pattern as it is known in the NLP world is shown in brackets if relevant. Please note that some of the patterns are similar to each other. Additional reading material is listed in the "Resources for Further Learning" section.

Pattern: Assumptions (mind reads).

Description: Claiming to know how someone is thinking or feeling.

Examples at work:

- "I know you're curious about how we can achieve our targets."
- "You're probably wondering why this is such an important meeting."

Pattern: Impersonal judgments (lost performatives).

Description: Making a judgment or assessment without saying who is doing the "judging."

Examples at work:

- "It's good that you're curious about how we can achieve our targets."
- "It's encouraging that you're so motivated."
- "That's right."

Pattern: Causations (cause and effect).

Description: Where one thing causes or leads to something else.

Examples at work:

- "Because you are here, you will learn lots of things."
- "If you attend the seminars, you will get your professional qualification."

Pattern: Equivalences (complex equivalence).

Description: Where one thing equals or means something else.

Examples at work:

- "Making these cold calls means you will hit your target."
- "Putting our best people on your account demonstrates our commitment to you."
- "This conversation is the start of a new relationship."

Pattern: Presuppositions.

Description: Where someone assumes that something is true.

Examples at work: "My clients are really interested in the great service I give them." This presupposes the person has clients, that they are interested in the service given, and that the service is great.

Pattern: Universals (universal quantifiers).

Description: Global words such as *all, every, each, none, no one, never, always*.

Examples at work:

- "You all want the best for the team."
- "We always strive to be responsive to our clients."
- "We are never knowingly undersold."

Pattern: Possibility, necessity (modal operators of possibility or necessity).

Description: Words that indicate rules, possibility, or impossibility.

Examples at work:

- "We can't afford to let the competition get ahead of us."
- "We need to keep innovating."
- "We mustn't fall into the trap of negative thinking."

Pattern: Frozen verbs (nominalizations).

Description: These are process words turned into an abstract noun: *commitment (to commit), decision (to decide), knowledge (to know), management (to manage), success (to succeed)*.

Examples at work:

- "Our commitment to you."
- "The decision has been made."
- "The management of the process was excellent."
- "My understanding is that we will proceed tomorrow."

Pattern: Unspecified verb.

Description: Where there is no evidence of how the verb is applied.

Examples at work:

- "He underestimated me."
- "We can't continue."

Pattern: Inserted questions (tag questions).

Description: Questions used to either emphasize or gain agreement.

Examples at work:

- "You can do that, can't you?"
- "You know what I mean, don't you?"
- "You've been happy with our products before, haven't you?"

Pattern: Simple deletions.

Description: Where so much information is left out that there could be various interpretations.

Examples at work: "I am happy." (With the weather, the results, the night's sleep I had?)

Pattern: Unspecified person/subject (lack of referential index).

Description: Where it is not clear who is the subject of the sentence.

Examples at work:

- "They arrived on time."
- "People say the results are improving."

Pattern: Unspecified comparisons (comparative deletions).

Description: Where something is compared to something else, without stating what it is compared to. Advertisers use this frequently.

Examples at work:

- "We try harder."
- "Our washing powder washed whiter."
- "We give you better value."
- "We offer you more."

Pattern: Pacing (pacing current experience). Please note that though this is not the same as "pacing" to build rapport (Chapter 5), it often has the effect of demonstrating that you are on the same wavelength as people, which will aid rapport-building.

Description: Making a statement (or series of statements) that is undeniably true. This is similar to the "yes set" used in selling, whereby sales people will seek to get the customer into the habit of saying "yes" with a view to then getting them to say "yes" to buying the product.

Examples at work:

- "You're sitting here, reading my book, learning about language patterns."

- (In a seminar) "You've come here, on this sunny/cloudy/dry/wet day, to learn about how to..."

Pattern: Impossible behaviors (sectional restriction violations).

Description: Where it is not possible for someone or something to have the response, or do the behavior.

Examples at work:

- "This house is crying out for a careful, loving owner." (Real estate agent)

- "This car loves to be driven firmly." (Sports car salesperson)

Putting it all together

Scenario: You are setting the scene for an important meeting about business development.

Good morning. Thank you all for coming. Some of you have traveled a long distance, some a shorter distance, to be here on time. I guess you're probably wondering why I asked you to come here on this sunny morning. And it's good that you're wondering, because this curiosity is the basis of how we can move forward to achieve the success and excellence that we all want to achieve. We all want more success and to be happy, don't we? And that's good, because in this economic environment we need to progress; people expect it. Successful companies never stand still; successful companies keep looking for ways forward.

Exercise 7.4

(approx. 5 minutes)

Reread the previous paragraph and notice how each of the abstract patterns was used at least once. (Check your answers against those in Appendix A.)

Applications in the workplace

These Milton Model abstract language patterns can be used in a variety of situations, such as:

- Selling, to bypass resistance.
- Presenting, to captivate the audience.
- Inspiring a team.
- Coaching a client.
- Running a training course.
- Advertising.

Here is a brief extract from the financial reports of a global motor manufacturer, talking about one of its guiding principles, to illustrate how even the most competitive businesses use these types of language constructs, whether knowingly or otherwise. I note, in brackets, the key Milton Model language pattern and/or the linguistic presupposition.

This principle is intended to keep the customer at the center of everything (universal) *we do* (unspecified verb), *and success* (frozen verb) *is* (equivalence) *pretty easy* (adjective) *to define. It means* (equivalence) *creating vehicles that people* (unspecified person) *desire, value and are proud to own. When* (if/when) *we get this right, it* (cause and effect) *transforms our reputation and the company's bottom line.*

Just look (awareness) *at the performance of the 20XX Model 1 in the United States and compare it to the Model 2 two years previously* (time)*. The average transaction price for Model 2 is about 28 percent* *higher, its projected resale value after three years is 32 percent higher and it gets 14 percent better highway fuel economy, according to EPA estimates. This is* (equivalence) *the kind of success* (existence) *we plan to replicate every* (universal) *opportunity we get.*

Exercise 7.5

Record, or watch on the Internet, an interview with a politician or business leader. Notice how often the interviewee uses Milton Model patterns (whether they realize it or not) and also notice the impact that each pattern has on you.

Let's now look at more detailed language.

Power questions

If you do not know how to ask the right question, you discover nothing.
—William Edwards Deming, American
business philosopher and consultant

Just as there is a language model using abstract language, there is a model that uses more specific language and which seeks to ask questions to uncover information that might have been deleted, distorted, or generalized. These questions are based on those that the eminent therapist, Virginia Satir (one of the other therapists modeled by Bandler and Grinder when developing NLP), asked when working with her clients; they can be easily used at work to uncover relevant information and will help you to ask the right kind of question at the right time. In NLP, these power questions are known as the "Meta Model" and, occasionally, as the "Precision Model."

Why power questions are so useful

Knowing the right kind of question to ask can be useful in many situations, for example:

- Selling, to uncover where the client's problems are and the related implications.
- Handling objections.
- Coaching, to get specific about the client's actions.
- Project planning.
- Meetings, to ensure that actions are agreed.

The questions

As we discussed in Chapter 2, every person deletes, distorts, and generalizes information. Given that we all do this, it is not surprising that the language we use reflects these internal filtering processes.

Let's consider the language patterns that fall into these three categories and the related Meta Model question. You will recognize the patterns from the Milton Model above. There is sometimes more than one possible response and these are listed below. Please use common sense when choosing which question to ask or, indeed, whether to ask a Meta Model question at all.

Distortions

Pattern: Assumptions (mind reads).

Example: "I know you're curious why I called the meeting."

Question/response: "How do you know I'm curious?"

Pattern: Impersonal judgments (lost performatives).

Example: "It's good to work hard."

Question/response:

- "Who says it's good?"
- "How do you know it's good?"

Pattern: Causations (cause and effect).

Example: "Presentations make me nervous."

Question/response: "How specifically do they make you feel nervous?"

Pattern: Equivalences (complex equivalence).

Example: "The client not returning my call means he's not interested."

Question/response:

- "How does the client not returning your call mean he's not interested?"
- "Have you ever not returned someone's call quickly and yet been interested?"(i.e. counter-example)

Pattern: Presuppositions.

Example: "If my boss was really interested in us, he would spend more time telling people how good we are."

Question/response:

- "How do you know your boss isn't interested in you?"
- "How do you know he doesn't tell people how good you are?"

Generalizations

Pattern: Universals (universal quantifiers).

Example:

- "We never buy from new suppliers."
- "We always get five quotes."

Question/response:

- "Never? Surely you must have bought from a new supplier at some time?"
- "Always? What would happen if you didn't?"

Look for counter-examples.

Pattern: Possibility/impossibility (modal operators of possibility/impossibility).

Example:

- "We can't buy from you."
- "I might work hard this week."

Question/response:

- "What would happen if you did?" or "What stops you?"
- "What would happen if you didn't?"

Pattern: Necessity (modal operators of necessity).

Example: "We have to expand abroad."

Question/response: "What would happen if we didn't?"

Pattern: Frozen verbs (nominalizations).

Example:

- "The communication is poor in this office."
- "I don't like his style of management."

Question/response:

- "How would you like people to communicate instead?" (turn the noun back into a process)
- "How would you like him to manage instead?"

Pattern: Unspecified verbs.

Example: "He ignored us."

Question/response: "What specifically did he do or not do that made you think he ignored you?"

Pattern: Simple deletions.

Example: "I'm upset."

Question/response: "About what, exactly?"

Pattern: Unspecified person/subject (lack of referential index).

Example: "They're not comfortable."

Question/response: "Who exactly isn't comfortable?"

Pattern: Unspecified comparisons (comparative deletions)

Example:

- "That's expensive."
- "Your competitors are better."

Question/response:

- "Compared to what?"
- "Better than who/what?"; "In what way exactly are they better?"

As you will have spotted, many of the Milton Model patterns have an associated Meta Model response because they are either end of the spectrum of language.

Because distortions tend to have the biggest impact on people's thinking, followed by generalizations and then deletions. If there is more than one type in a sentence challenge the distortions before generalizations, and generalizations before deletions.

Tip 7.2

Please be clear about the purpose of asking a power question. I have seen people use these questions as a way to annoy other people and hijack a discussion, which had no tangible benefit for anyone.

Exercise 7.6

Revisit the interview with a politician or business leader mentioned in Exercise 7.5. Listen to the questions that the interviewer is asking to obtain information. With your knowledge now, what questions would you ask instead? Which statements made by the politician or business leader would you challenge, and using which question(s)?

Applications of power questions

There are numerous work applications:

- Interviewing candidates, to find out what they actually did in previous roles.
- Interviewing prospective employers, to find out exactly what the role entails.
- Selling, to find out exactly what the prospect wants and how they would know that they had it.
- Managing and coaching, to pin down employees/clients about what they are going to do and when.
- Project planning and actions from meetings, to agree who exactly will do what and by when.
- Contracts and negotiations, to ensure that the details are as you want.

Let's now move on to the final language topic.

Stories, analogies, and metaphors

The use of stories, analogies, and metaphors can be an effective way to:

- Illustrate and explain the point you are making to staff, clients, and interviewers.
- Overcome resistance to your ideas from staff, prospects, customers, and coaching clients.
- Help your audience to remember the points you are making at meetings and presentations.
- Engage your audience even more when making presentations.

Stories and metaphors are effective because our "automatic response" process (i.e. our unconscious mind) is like that of a young child; those of us who have been around young children know how engaged they are when you tell them stories, as it allows their mind to create a story inside their own head. Many people can remember fairy tales and those stories their grandparents told them when they were young, yet they might not be able to remember much about what happened at a meeting a few weeks ago.

Here are some examples of how you can use metaphors:

- Telling a story or giving an example of how you overcame a challenge that is similar to the one that is being faced by the person you are speaking to (e.g. client, colleague, supplier).

- Telling a story about how someone else overcame the challenge. This is sometimes more effective than telling a story about your-self, because it is more detached from the situation. The story could be about someone you know, such as another client, or a well-known situation in the public arena, or it can be a fable.

- Telling a story about how another client used your services as a way to overcome sales objections. You will have noticed that I use examples and stories in this book to illustrate the points I am making.

Tip 7.3

Pay attention to speakers whom you find engaging and notice how they use stories to explain their ideas. Practice the use of relevant stories when at relatively unimportant meetings and notice the impact on the listener(s). Once you feel comfortable with using stories, then, if appropriate, use them at more important meetings.

Part III

Some Specific NLP Techniques

Part III looks at some of the NLP techniques and models that you can use in the workplace.

Chapter 8 looks at a model that can be used to structure the way you think about situations and inform you about how to make changes that will lead to greater levels of congruence and alignment, both individually and organizationally.

Chapter 9 describes how you can alter the way you think about situations that might previously have challenged you or where you respond in unhelpful ways.

Chapter 10 covers how to get into a useful state, almost at the click of your fingers, and how to use these principles at work.

Chapter 11 covers an extremely useful technique that will help you see other perspectives and which can be used in a variety of business situations.

Chapter 12 discusses how to influence in conversation the way colleagues and clients perceive situations and how to turn negatives into positives.

Chapter 13 follows on from the principles of Chapter 12 and explains methods to change other people's beliefs during conversation.

A word about NLP "interventions"

Part III describes how to use various NLP techniques to make changes to the way you think and feel about a situation. In NLP, we call these techniques "interventions."

Throughout the whole process of any intervention, it is **essential** to ensure that:

- You are in rapport with the person(s) you are interacting with (Chapter 5).

- You use sensory acuity to calibrate how the other person(s) is/are feeling (Chapter 5).

You will also find it extremely useful to bear in mind, and use where appropriate, representational systems, predicates and eye patterns (Chapter 6) and relevant aspects of the different language models (Chapter 7).

Before starting the intervention, I often find it useful to ask my clients to rank their current situation or response on a scale of 1 to 10, and their desired situation on the same scale, and how they would know in 10 to 20 minutes (the typical duration of interventions) that they were at the desired score and had achieved what they wanted from the exercise. By way of an example, if a client is nervous about going for an interview, they may feel 4 out of 10 confident, and would like to feel 9 or 10, and they would know that they would be feeling 9 out of 10 if the knot they have in their stomach at the thought of the interview disappeared, and if they were looking forward to the interview. This scaling exercise is a useful way to focus your mind and to provide a check to know that the intervention has worked.

One of the essential aspects of doing interventions is that the consequences of making the change to your thinking, feeling, and hence behaviors are fully considered beforehand. This is known as doing an "ecology check." You learned about "ecology" from "SMARTER" goals in Chapter 4; the four ecology questions (page 56) can be extremely useful.

I recommend that you do ecology checks by asking yourself (or your "client" if you are coaching or managing them) the following questions:

- Are there any negative consequences whatsoever about making the change that will result from the intervention? (For example, following on from the example above, could feeling 10 out of 10 confident about the interview lead to a blasé attitude?) Ideally there should be no negative consequences (see below).

- What are the positive consequences? List or think of as many as you can, starting with the professional impact and then, if possible, the knock-on benefits, for example, on your home life and health. The more you can identify, the more successful the intervention is likely to be, because you will be more motivated to do it. You can use the four ecology questions instead of, or in addition to, the questions about negative/positive consequences.

- On a scale of 0 to 100 percent, where 0 percent means you don't want to do this and 100 percent means you absolutely do want to make the changes, how much do you want to do it? My suggestion is to proceed only if it's 100 percent.

Occasionally there will be minor negative consequences of doing the intervention (for example, doing well in an interview might mean a temporary increase in workload or pressure if you get the job or promotion). If this is the case, check that the benefits significantly outweigh the minor downsides.

Some advice

As indicated in the "eye patterns" section of Chapter 6, people often move their eyes to different areas, or stare ahead, when thinking and searching for information internally. Though sitting opposite someone in typical working situations is commonplace (subject to any cultural factors), when guiding people through the NLP processes covered in Chapters 8 to 11, it is normally helpful to them if you are either at their side or at an angle to them, as opposed to being directly in front of them.

Other prerequisites for NLP interventions

Here are some additional points, already made in the Introduction, of which I would like to remind you. These points are relevant before doing any NLP intervention in a coaching or "guiding" context.

Firstly, especially when you are new to NLP, best results are gained by following the process as written, especially where you are doing this by yourself or guiding a colleague or coaching a client through the process. As you become more familiar with the technique and have had some professional NLP training, you can be a little more flexible.

Secondly, I strongly recommend that you read the process through more than once before doing the technique and if you use it with someone else, read it as many times as you require so that you are absolutely clear as to how to do it.

Finally, these techniques are to be used with individuals only as a coaching, mentoring, or management tool for improving work performance, not as a form of psychotherapy unless you are specifically trained in psychotherapy.

Organizational and Personal Alignment

Walking your talk

Sir, I'm helping to put a man on the moon.
—A janitor at NASA, in response to President J. F. Kennedy
asking him what he did at NASA

Individuals and organizations tend to function more productively if there is an internal congruence or alignment about what they are doing. For example, are they being true to themselves and what's really important to them? In this chapter, we will be covering a model that will help both you as an individual and your organization to be able to become even more congruent, as well as providing a structure for approaching challenges and problems. The model is known in NLP as the "Neurological Levels" model.

Why is this model so useful?

You can use the model in several ways:

- As a business leader, manager, or consultant, to analyze the types of management action required to make the desired change to an organization's performance, structure, or culture.

- As a manager or coach, to analyze the types of intervention required for individual performance improvement.

- As a salesperson, to gain a better understanding of the motivation behind a purchase.

- As a coach, to help someone become a more effective leader or manager.
- As an individual, to gain greater clarity and sense of purpose, or to coach/manage someone to do this.
- To give and receive feedback effectively.

The Neurological Levels model

The model is based on work done by Robert Dilts and the anthropologist, Gregory Bateson (as a student, Dilts worked with Bandler and Grinder, and Bateson provided guidance to all of them in the early days of NLP's development). It considers different levels of thinking and perception as shown in Diagram 8.1.

Each level is explained in the following sections and can apply either to organizations or to individuals. Each level has an implied question as shown in the diagram.

Diagram 8.1

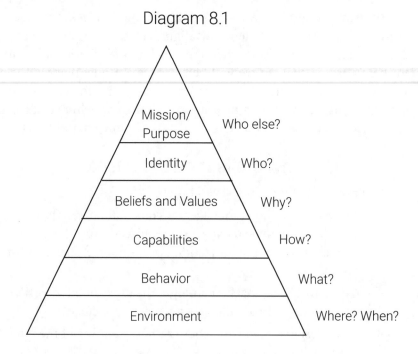

Mission/purpose

This relates to your (or your organization's) concept of *who else* is affected by your (or its) actions. Who else are you (is it) serving? What is your (its) legacy? An organization might want to consider its impact on anything from the local community through to the whole world. You might recognize that your actions impact on a wide range of people. The theory of "six degrees of separation" indicates that we are six contacts away from every single person in the world, so what you do (or what your organization does) will impact people whom you might never actually meet.

In some schools of NLP, mission/purpose is treated as being outside the Neurological Levels model and is sometimes referred to as "beyond identity."

Identity

This relates to your sense of self, *who* you are. An organization will often cultivate brand identity, so that when consumers think of it, they immediately feel that they know who the organization is. You will have a sense of who you are as a person and possibly have a different sense of identity in different contexts (e.g. manager at work, parent at home). Some people use metaphors or analogies to describe themselves in certain situations ("I'm like a tiger/lion/superwoman").

Beliefs and values

We touched on these to some degree in Chapter 2. These points, although different from each other, are often linked, and they form the basis for our motivation—*why* we do something.

Beliefs are convictions we hold as being true, and these shape our behaviors. If you believe you can present well, you will have a different response to being asked to make a presentation compared to someone who believes they cannot present well. We will look at beliefs more closely in Chapter 13.

Values are those things that are important to us, or they can be what we want, or look for, in a particular context. Organizations often display their values in reception, on their Website, and on literature; these can act as guiding principles as to how organizations treat staff and customers. Individuals have values in all areas of life, and if you reflect on it for a moment, you will become aware of what is important to you about, for example, your career. Knowing your own career values will help you to make better choices; knowing other people's values will help you to influence them. We will look at values more closely in Chapter 14.

Capabilities

This relates to *how* things get done, including the skills, abilities, and qualities organizations require and which individuals have. They include strategies used.

Behaviors

This is *what* individuals and organizations actually do. Behaviors can usually be seen or heard and are tangible. HR professionals often combine behaviors and capabilities under the umbrella of "competencies," and they are often used as a framework for improving performance and planning training needs, both for individuals and for organizations.

Environment

This relates to *where* something takes place, such as how the work environment looks and feels. It can also be linked to *when* something takes place.

Some key principles about the Neurological Levels model

Although not directly linked to the Hierarchy of Ideas covered in Chapter 7, starting with environment, each of the levels is a higher level of abstraction than the previous one.

As a general principle, the higher levels have greater influence and power than the lower levels. Changing your sense of identity will normally have a greater impact than changing the color of the office wallpaper (environment).

Similarly, it is normally harder to change the higher levels: changing the way you greet people (behavior) is probably easier than changing what you believe.

For you personally, the more each of the levels align with each other, the more congruent and effective you will be, and the more you will be "walking your talk," which will usually lead to your achieving more and having a greater sense of well-being. This is especially true if you have a strong sense of purpose. Great leaders, such as Nelson Mandela, Martin Luther King, and Winston Churchill, all had a strong sense of what they wanted, especially in respect of topics they felt passionately about (ending apartheid, starting the civil rights movement, and leading Britain through the Second World War respectively). Successful business leaders such as Henry Ford (Ford Motor Company), Jack Welsh (General Electric), Anita Roddick (The Body Shop), and Steve Jobs (Apple) are examples of successful business people who had a clear sense of purpose and truly believed in what they were doing and learned the necessary skills to execute their plans successfully.

The same principle applies to organizations. To the extent that organizations walk their talk and encourage the same degree of congruence amongst staff, great results can happen (please refer to the NASA quote at the start of this chapter). In my career, initially as a management consultant and more recently as a trainer and coach, I have seen some organizations that do walk their talk, and unfortunately many other organizations that espouse certain values in print but where the directors and senior managers do not actually operate as if those values were in place. Therefore, the extent to which you set business goals that align with the Neurological Levels will create a powerful recipe for success at work.

Tip 8.1

Because the higher levels are more important and significant than the lower levels, provided that you have a strong enough sense of purpose/mission, identity, beliefs, and values, you will find a way to achieve what you want, even if you don't have the competencies yet or even if the environment is not perfect.

Using the Neurological Levels model to gain alignment

Let's look at how you can use the model, both individually and as an organization, to gain greater alignment at work. Here is a selection of key questions in both contexts.

Individuals

Mission/Purpose. Who are you serving in your role? Who else is impacted by those people? What is your purpose in your work/ business?

Identity. Who are you in your work? What is your sense of self at work? This could be one "I am..." statement or several. Does your sense of self align with your purpose?

Beliefs and values. What do you believe about your work (and/or employer)? What is important to you about your work? What do you believe about your colleagues? What beliefs would be useful for you to adopt? Do your beliefs and values align with and support your identity and purpose?

Capabilities. What skills do you have that are relevant to your role? Which are your key skills? Which ones would you like to improve or acquire? How will you do that? Do your skills support what you want to achieve and your purpose?

Behaviors. Which behaviors do you exhibit at work? Which really support your success and which ones (if any) in some way hinder it?

Environment: Is your environment representative of who you are and what you want to achieve? What aspects of your environment support you and which hinder you?

Organizations

Good business leaders create a vision, articulate the vision, passionately own the vision, and relentlessly drive it to completion.

—Jack Welsh, Chairman and CEO of General Electric from 1981 to 2001

Mission/Purpose. Who is your organization serving? What is its purpose and mission? Who else is impacted by the organization's actions?

Identity. Who is the organization? How does it see itself? How do its customers and employees see it? Is it aligned with the mission/purpose?

Beliefs and values. What does the organization value? What does it stand for? What is important to it about how it interacts with the world, including employees and customers? Do its behaviors always reflect this? What does it believe about itself, its products, its customers, and employees?

Capabilities. What skills are important to achieve the organisation's goals? To what extent does it have these skills at the moment?

Behaviors. What does the organization do? Which behaviors help it to achieve its goals? Which behaviors hinder it?

Environment. Does the environment reflect who the organization is and what it wants to achieve? Which aspects of the environment support its staff to excel and which ones hinder them? Which geographic area(s) could it expand into?

Exercise 8.1

If you are relatively senior in your organization (including running your own business) or run a department, review your organization's or department's performance in the light of the Neurological Levels model. Consider the following questions:

- To what extent are all the levels in alignment and supporting each other?
- Are the publicized values acted on in reality, especially when there is some stress or during very busy periods?
- Is the working environment conducive to excellent work and in accordance with the image you portray publicly?
- Are your staff adequately trained to deliver on the organization's mission?

What changes could you make or recommend? Even if you are not in a senior position, running a business or department, you could still benefit from doing this exercise because you would develop a greater understanding of the organization or business. Depending on the organization you work for and the individuals concerned, you might find that your managers or directors are open to discussing it and hearing your thoughts, which might have career benefits.

Other applications of the Neurological Levels model

Organizational change: When making a culture change, and seeking to capture the hearts and minds (i.e. some of the higher levels), it is important to remember to address change at each level. For example, changing the organization's purpose and mission, without addressing the beliefs and values of staff, or their capabilities, is unlikely to lead to a successful change in culture.

Leadership development: You can use the Neurological Levels model to develop leadership skills, as shown in the following exercise.

> *Management is about doing things right;*
> *leadership is about doing the right things.*

—Peter F. Drucker, management-development author and expert

Exercise 8.2

(approx. 10–15 minutes)

Mark out each of the six levels on the floor in a line. Starting at environment and working up each of the levels in turn, ask yourself (or your colleague/client if you are a manager or business coach) the following questions at the respective level.

Environment: Where do you lead?

Behaviors: Which behaviors do you exhibit as a leader? What do you do?

Capabilities: What skills and abilities do you have as a leader? How do you lead?

Beliefs and values: What is important to you as a leader? What do you believe as a leader?

Identity: Who are you as a leader? What's your sense of self as a leader?

Mission/Purpose: Who else are you serving as a leader? Who else is impacted when you lead?

At mission/purpose, pause and really consider who else you are serving in your role as a leader or manager, and then turn round and look back along the five levels, noticing any insights you might have. Then return to each of the levels in turn as follows.

Identity: Who are you *now* as a leader? What's your sense of self *now* as a leader?

Beliefs and values: What is important to you *now* as a leader? What do you believe *now* as a leader?

Capabilities: What skills and abilities do you have as a leader? What skills would you like to learn/acquire?

Behaviors: Which behaviors do you exhibit as a leader? Which behaviors would you like to change? Which behaviors would you like to learn/adopt?

Environment: Where do you lead? Where else would you like to lead?

After returning to environment, move to the side and step back to notice what you have learned and what action(s) you will take.

Diagram 8.2 summarizes the exercise.

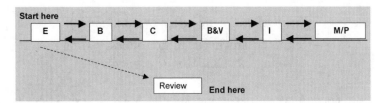

You can also use this exercise in different contexts apart from leadership, for example, to improve your ability as a manager or salesperson.

Giving and receiving feedback: One of the NLP Presuppositions is that people are doing the best they can, and that their behaviors do not represent their identity. From the Neurological Levels model, it is important as a manager to recognize that even if someone's behaviors might seem unusual or unhelpful, this is not who they are as a person (identity), and that it is far easier to change behaviors than to change a person. Another useful NLP Presupposition is that there is no failure, only feedback.

A really useful feedback model is as follows:

- What did your colleague do well? Speak about behaviors (such as "you drew lots of relevant flipchart diagrams") rather than identity statements (such as "you are an excellent presenter") so that the colleague knows what to repeat.

- What are one or two things (i.e. **behaviors**) that they could do to make it even better? Stay at behavioral level, as behaviors are relatively easy to change. "Keep eye contact" is something a colleague can work on. "You can't deliver to a large group" (capability level), or even worse, "you're a nervous presenter" (identity level) doesn't help a colleague know what to do and it can be disempowering.

- Finish with an overall positive comment, either at behavioral, capability, or even identity level ("you are a good presenter").

When receiving feedback, if it is given at behavioral level, receive it at behavioral level and resist any possible reflex action to distort it to be at capability or identity level, such as "I'm a bad presenter" (identity), or "I don't make the audience feel comfortable" (capability).

Feedback is the breakfast of champions.
—Kenneth Blanchard, author of best-selling
book *The One Minute Manager*

Selling: certain consumer items, such as jewelry, sports cars, and designer clothes, could be purchased by someone seeking to enhance their sense of identity as opposed to purely for certain environments or to be purely functional (behavior). As a salesperson, if you can tune in to this, you can use the knowledge to sell at the most relevant level.

Problem solving (consultant, coach, manager): when faced with a challenge or problem, seek to identify at which Neurological Level the problem is, and then address it at least at that level, or possibly a higher level. For example, let's assume you have a colleague who is not effective when chairing meetings. If they simply do not know which behaviors to exhibit, or do not have the necessary skills (i.e. behavior and capability levels), then sending them on a training course to learn new competencies will probably help, especially if the course in some way addresses the importance of chairing a meeting well (values). If, however, they think that they are not the sort of person to chair meetings (identity), then sending them on the training course will be a waste of time and money. Coaching to address their sense of identity and even to realize how chairing the meeting could fit in with their own sense of purpose would be more effective.

9

Managing Your Thoughts

How to change the way you think

If you change the way you look at things, the things you look at will change.
—Dr. Wayne Dyer, author

As we covered in Chapter 2, external events and situations create "internal representations" (i.e. thoughts) inside people's heads. These thoughts take the form of pictures, sounds (including self-talk), and feelings; by changing certain aspects of these three representational systems relating to the experience, you can change the way you think about a situation or event, which in turn changes the way you respond. This chapter covers how to do this. The technique you will learn is relevant for individuals rather than for organizations, although usually if individual employees improve performance, there are benefits for the organization.

Why is this so useful?

You can use this approach to help yourself in several ways:

- To feel more confident about interviews, presentations, and meetings with important clients or colleagues.

- To feel more positive about certain work activities that you might not necessarily like, such as writing reports, cold calling, or submitting work to deadlines. (One student on an NLP Practitioner course won $750,000 of business from a blue-chip company by using this process for cold calling.)

- To feel comfortable around people who you might have pre-viously felt intimidated by because of their personality or job title.

Background

As you remember from Chapters 2 and 6, in NLP we refer to our senses as "representational systems." They are also known as "modalities." When people think of a situation, they will instantly have either a picture of it, sounds associated with it, or feelings about it; usually the internal represen-tation will be in one, two, or even three of these modalities and will often happen so automatically that they will not be aware of it. If we take just the visual modality for a moment, the picture will have certain qualities, such as size (big, medium, or small), brightness (bright or dim), and movement (still, slow, medium, or fast). These finer distinctions of the modalities are called "submodalities" and their function is to help us interpret and give meaning to the experience. For example, submodalities inform us whether we like or dislike an activity (such as cold calling or chairing meetings). By changing the submodalities, the experience will change.

Several books have been written about submodalities alone; it is a topic that requires professionally supervised training before you can use it fully and with other people. In this book, we will cover some of the key elements so that you can use submodalities for yourself at work.

Please note that, as with all topics covered in this book, submodalities are to be used for relatively minor situations and responses, *not* major emo-tional issues like raging anger or phobias.

A little more about submodalities

You will probably have heard people use phrases at work such as:

- "Put that idea to one side."
- "The dim and distant past."
- "The picture is fuzzy."
- "I hear you loud and clear."
- "This is a big problem weighing heavily on my shoulders."

Each of these phrases indicates some key submodalities that the speak-er is using, even though the speaker almost certainly doesn't realize it.

Table 9.1 shows a list of the main submodalities.

Table 9.1

Visual	Auditory	Kinesthetic
Size (big, small, medium)	Location (left, right, front, back)	Location (chest, stomach, throat, etc.)
Location in your visual field (high/low, left/center/right)	Direction of movement (toward you, away from you, clockwise/counterclockwise)	Size of feeling
Brightness (bright/dim)	Volume (loud/soft)	Shape
Distance (near/far)	Pitch (high/low)	Intensity of feeling
Looking through your own eyes or seeing yourself*	Speed (fast/slow)	Movement (speed)
Color or black and white	Internal or external	Vibration
Degree of Focus	Pauses	Texture (rough/smooth)
Steady/changing focus	Rhythm	Weight
3D or Flat	Duration of the sound	Temperature
Framed or panoramic	Uniqueness of the sound	Pressure (high/low)
Still/moving (if moving, fast/normal/slow?)		

Looking through your own eyes is known as "associated"; seeing yourself in the picture is known as "dissociated."

Some of the submodalities are on a spectrum (known as "analogue"), such as brightness (bright as the sun, dim as a coal mine, or anything in between) and volume (almost silent to almost deafening), and some are either/or (known as "digital"), for example, three dimensional or flat, associated or dissociated.

When you change certain submodalities, it will make little or no difference to the way you feel about the situation or event because, for you, when thinking about the specific situation these submodalities are not important. When you change others, it will make a difference (either positive or negative)—these are called "critical" submodalities. There will be one or two submodalities that, when you change them, will be so important that all the other submodalities will change and your experience of the situation will change significantly; these are called "driver" submodalities. Though there are some submodalities that tend to be significant for most people, it is important to recognize that:

- You are unique and the specific submodalities that impact you might be different from those for someone else.

- The driver or critical submodalities for any given situation in which you are involved might be different from those for another situation in which you are involved, so treat each situation uniquely.

Exercise 9.1

(approx. 5 minutes)

As an introduction to submodalities, choose a pleasant work experience, either a past positive work memory or a situation you are looking forward to or a work task you like doing. As you think of the event, get a picture of it in your mind, and notice the main submodality aspects (visual and, if relevant, auditory and kinaesthetic) of the events (review Table 9.1 beforehand). Make a note quickly of any submodalities that you particularly notice.

Making a note of submodalities is known as "eliciting" submodalities.

Tip 9.1

Elicit submodalities as quickly as possible and resist any possible temptation to over-analyze. By their very nature, submodalities "occur" almost instantly as we think about a particular topic; doing this quickly helps you to elicit the submodalities as they truly are.

Using submodalities

There are two main methods of using submodalities.

Method 1

This is called "mapping across." In essence, you change the critical submodalities of the current, undesired response into those of the desired response. This has the effect of giving the current response the same submodalities, and therefore the same meaning, as the desired response.

To illustrate this, I will use the example of a business consultant who wanted to be able to make cold calls comfortably (someone who had the capability, but just didn't feel comfortable doing it).

Preparation phase:

1. Identify a current undesired response (e.g. feeling uncomfortable at the thought of making a cold call). If it helps, score on a scale of 1–10 how comfortable you feel about doing it (1 is very uncomfortable, 10 is very comfortable).

2. Decide what your ideal score would be and identify a similar type of work activity where your responses are close to that score, that is, the desired response (e.g. phoning a work colleague). It is essential to pick a topic in the same context as the undesired response; in this case, both involve making work phone calls.

3. Do the ecology check (see page 56) to ensure that there are no (or only minor) negative consequences of responding to cold

calling in the same way as you respond to—in this example, calling colleagues, and that there are significant benefits (which far outweigh any possible drawbacks).

Intervention:

1. Think of "cold calling," make a picture, and then, using the following Table 9.2, *very quickly* (remember Tip 9.1) make a note of the main visual submodalities in column 1. Ask yourself if there are any sounds that are important and, if so, elicit and make a note of the auditory submodalities. Repeat with the kinesthetic submodalities. I suggest that you use abbreviations where possible to help you do this quickly (e.g. "B" for "black and white").

2. Clear your mind and then repeat the process, this time with "calling a colleague" rather than "cold calling," and make a note of the main submodalities in column 2.

3. Mark (with an asterisk) any differences between the two sets of submodalities. This is known in NLP as "contrastive analysis."

4. Bring back to mind the picture of cold calling. For the submodalities that are different (i.e. the critical submodalities), one by one, change each "cold calling" submodality to be the same as the corresponding one for "calling a colleague." For example, if the "cold calling" picture is small and the "calling a colleague" picture is large, make the "cold calling" picture large in your mind. Continue this process quickly with all submodalities marked (with an asterisk). You might find that there are one or two submodalities that, when you change them, cause the others to change too. This is because these are "driver" submodalities.

5. Check how you feel about cold calling (it should now be the same as that for calling a colleague). Then internally lock into place the submodality changes you have just made. Some people do this visually, by visualizing the changes being locked. Others do this in an auditory way, perhaps by imagining the sound of a food container being closed, or in a kinaesthetic way by, for example, imagining the feel of tying something into place. Do it in a way that works effectively for you.

6. Mentally rehearse making cold calls (i.e. the desired new behavior) in several scenarios. This is known as "future pacing" when, having just used the NLP technique, you envisage yourself in the future situation (and several different scenarios of these future situations) and notice how your responses are different now compared to how they were. Many successful business people and athletes use this type of visualization of future scenarios.

Table 9.2

Visual	1	2
Black and white or color		
Near or far		
Bright or dim		
Location		
Size of picture		
Associated/dissociated		
Focused or defocused		
Focus (changing/steady)		
Framed or panoramic		
Movie or still		
Movie—fast/normal/slow		
3D or flat		
Auditory (are there any sounds that are important?)		
Location		
Direction		
Internal or external		
Loud or soft		
Fast or slow		
Pitch (high/low)		
Timbre—clear/raspy		
Pauses		

Cadence/rhythm		
Duration		
Uniqueness of sound		
Kinesthetic (are there any feelings that are important?)		
Location		
Size		
Shape		
Intensity (high/low)		
Steady		
Still/moving		
Fast/slow		
Duration (short/long)		
Humidity (dry/wet)		
Vibration		
Hot/cold		
Pressure? (high/low)		
Texture (rough/smooth)		
Heavy/light		

Method 2

This can be quicker and involves a slightly more "try it and see" approach. The preparation phase is the same as in the first method above.

Intervention:

1. Think of the current undesired response (nerves about cold calling).

2. Make a picture of "cold calling" and change one visual submodality, and notice whether it makes it better, worse, or whether there is no change. If there is no change, change it back to how it was. If you chose a digital submodality (such as color/black and white, or three dimensional/flat) and it makes it worse, change it back to how it was. If changing an analogue submodality (such as distance, size, or brightness) makes it worse, change it to the opposite extreme and notice the impact. For example, if

making the picture smaller makes your response worse, return it to the size it was and then make it bigger.

3. Retain any positive submodality changes and keep going until your score/response is how you want it to be. Then internally lock into place the submodality changes you have just made.

4. Mentally rehearse (future pace) making cold calls (i.e. the desired new behavior) in several scenarios. Because this is a "try it and see" approach, I suggest that you start with the following submodalities (Table 9.3) as these tend to be more powerful, before moving on to the others if required.

Table 9.3

Visual	Auditory	Kinesthetic
Size	Location	Location
Location	Direction of movement	Size
Brightness		Shape
Distance	Volume (loud/soft)	Intensity of feeling
Associated/dissociated	Speed (fast/slow)	Movement (speed)
		Texture (rough/smooth)
		Temperature

Tip 9.2

Generally, making the following submodality changes will **increase** the impact of a situation (i.e. make it more pleasant if it is a pleasant experience and vice versa):

• Making pictures bigger, brighter, closer, more focused, three dimensional, associated, in color, and higher.

• Making sounds come toward you, louder (not too loud).

• Making feelings bigger, smoother, warmer (not too hot), have greater intensity.

Generally, the reverse will be true to lessen the impact.

Exercise 9.2

(approx 5–15 minutes)

Pick a situation or response that you have at work that you would like to change (see the "Why is this so useful?" section on page 135 for some ideas). Choose one of the two methods outlined in the previous section and do this exercise. Method 1 tends to be slightly more thorough as it targets specific sub-modality changes, although it might take a little longer because you are working with two sets of submodalities. Method 2 is more random, as you are guessing which submodalities are important. Once you become more familiar with working with your submodalities, you will be better able to know which ones are likely to be "critical" or "driver" submodalities, and hence be able to start with those, which can speed up the process.

A word about "association" and "dissociation"

One of the more useful submodalities is "association/dissociation." As a general rule, when people are associated into an event (i.e. seeing, hearing, and feeling it as if it were happening right now), they feel it much more than if they are dissociated from it (i.e. as if it were happening on a TV or cinema screen). If you happen to think of a situation that causes you some negative feelings, such as feeling overwhelmed or nervous, one thing you can do to gain a more balanced perspective is to step back from the situation so that you can see yourself in it. From this dissociated position, you can take a more considered view of what to do and how to respond.

Applications of submodalities at work

We have touched on various situations where this technique can be useful. Other applications include the following:

- **Goal setting:** You can change the submodalities to make your goal even more compelling. Also, when thinking about future work goals, once you have associated into achieving the goal and felt how good it is, it is often more compelling and motivating to then make the picture slightly dissociated so that you can see yourself achieving the goal rather than associated having already achieved it, which could cause a loss of motivation.

- **Selling and advertising:** You can use some of the language of submodalities, linked to predicates, to make your product more appealing—for example, "if you look closely at our new product" ("closely" implies that the picture is near).

- **Presentations, interviews, meetings, or any work situation where you feel less positive than you would like:** Adjust the submodalities when you think of the situation to make the feeling just right for you.

10

The Right State

How to create it for you and others

You cannot control what happens to you, but you can control your attitude towards what happens to you, and in that you will be mastering change rather than allowing it to master you.
—Brian Tracy, author, entrepreneur, and motivational speaker

In the last chapter, we looked at how you can change your internal representations to lead to changes in behaviors and results. In this chapter, we will be covering how to change your state and influence other people's states, which as you will remember from the Communication Model, is another way to change behaviors and results. The NLP term for managing state is known as "anchoring."

Why is anchoring so useful?

Being able to change your own state and influence other people's states is useful before and during many work situations where you might feel a little nervous or anxious, including:

- Interviews, both as interviewer and interviewee.
- Presentations.
- Negotiations.
- Meetings.
- Appraisals.

The process of setting an anchor for yourself, so that you can get into the right state whenever you want to, typically takes 10–15 minutes, which is a small investment of time for such a large benefit. Anchoring can also be used where you want to help other people to access and feel certain states, such as:

- Managing people regarding the previous activities.
- Advertising and marketing.
- Selling.

Please note that, as with submodalities, anchoring is to be used in situations where the current "problem" is relatively minor and related to specific situations. Feeling a little anxious before an interview is relatively common. Feeling wild panic or feeling anxious all the time is outside the scope of this book.

An overview of anchoring

An anchor is defined in NLP as "a stimulus that leads to a response in other people or yourself." One of the earliest and best-known exponents of anchoring was the Russian physiologist Ivan Pavlov, whose famous experiment with dogs in 1904 showed how they could be trained to respond to certain preset stimuli. Anchoring could be regarded as an entirely natural human response, and anchors can be set using any or all of the representational systems. You automatically respond (positively or negatively) to a variety of events, such as:

- The sound of your favorite upbeat music or, at work, the voice of your boss or most important customer.
- The sight of your best friend's face or, at work, seeing the managing director walk into the building.
- The smell of freshly ground coffee or, at work, the perfume/aftershave of your boss.
- The feel of your favorite freshly ironed shirt or blouse as you get dressed for an important interview.
- The taste of apple pie like your grandmother used to make.

One of the principles of anchoring is that you can create your own stimulus–response mechanisms for yourself, and even create or evoke states in other people. Diagram 10.1 shows this.

If you remember a time when you felt, for example, really excited and relive that specific event, your state will intensify, reach a peak (typically for 5–15 seconds), and then you will return to your everyday base-line state (shown by the inverted U in Diagram 10.1). If you link the peak of the state (shown by the think line) to a specific movement, such as squeezing your thumb and index finger together, and repeat this process a few times, the state ("excitement" in this case) and the movement will become neurologically linked, so that if you repeat the thumb-finger movement before or during a business meeting, you will feel in the state you have anchored (i.e. excited).

Diagram 10.1

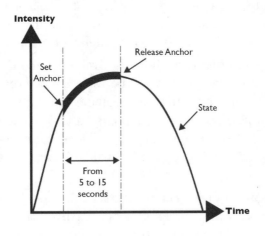

How to create an anchor for yourself

We will now move on to look at how you can set your own anchor for use in the type of work situations mentioned earlier, or to guide someone else through the process.

Tip 10.1

Please read the next two sections thoroughly and probably more than once, so that you are very clear how to do the process before actually setting the anchor in yourself or someone else. Please refer to the process and follow the process closely so that you get the desired result from the anchoring technique.

The five keys to anchoring

Before we discuss how to actually set an anchor, it's important to discuss the five key points to successful anchoring.

1. **Intensity:** When you "fire" (i.e. activate or trigger) the anchor before or during the interview (for example), it will only be as strong as the experiences you used when setting the anchor originally. So, assuming that you want to be able to feel highly confident (for example), then when you do the anchoring process use situations when you felt highly or intensely confident.

2. **Timing:** In order to anchor effectively, it is important that you capture the peak of the state (between the two vertical lines in Diagram 10.1) by setting or applying the anchor as the state nears its peak (i.e. at its most intense) and then releasing the anchor just after the peak. Typically the peak lasts 5–15 seconds, although depending on the individual it can vary from one or two seconds to a minute.

3. **Uniqueness of the anchor:** The stimulus should be unique so that it is easy to set and will not be fired/activated accidentally. Anchors on the palm of the hand, for example, will be constantly triggered when shaking hands at work and will probably lose their impact, whereas squeezing the tip of your thumb and index finger on your left hand or squeezing a specific finger knuckle are probably unique movements for most people.

4. **Replicability of the anchor:** It is essential that you can fire the anchor whenever you need to. Holding your left ankle with your right hand is probably unique but not replicable before or during an interview or presentation. Pressing your thumb and index finger together or touching a specific knuckle are probably replicable during most situations: other people present would probably not notice your doing it and, even if they did, would not think twice about it.

5. **Number of times the anchoring is done:** When doing the anchoring process, typically doing it between four and six times will be more powerful and long-lasting compared to doing it once or twice.

A useful mnemonic to remember these key points is **ITURN**.

The seven steps to anchoring

There are seven steps to setting an anchor. The process is sometimes known as setting a "resource anchor."

1. **Ensure you are clear about the anchoring process** (i.e. these seven steps and the five keys) and decide on the desired state(s) to be anchored—for example, confident, motivated, powerful (assume that confident is the desired state for this exercise)— and how you will anchor it. I suggest that you use a kinesthetic anchor such as squeezing your finger and thumb together or squeezing a knuckle. Physical movements tend to be more effective and replicable, although it is possible to make an internal sound or see an image in your mind. Remember the "R" of ITURN—it needs to be replicable. An external sound or a picture might not always be available to you. Do an ecology check (see page 56) to ensure that it is appropriate for you to have this resource anchor.

2. **Recall a vivid past experience** of an event where you felt one of these desired states. Pick one feeling/emotion at a time (e.g. confident) and then one past experience that relates to that emotion. If for some reason you cannot think of a time when you felt, for example, confident, give yourself a little time. Sometimes people cannot immediately come up with a situation but when they think of one, other memories start flooding back. If that does not work, pretend! Our unconscious mind does not know the difference between an actual event and a vividly imagined one.

3. **Make sure you are really associated into that event,** in other words, you are reliving it as if you were there right now, not merely thinking about it. See what you are seeing (i.e. as if it

were happening right now), hear what you are hearing and really feel the feelings of being totally confident.

4. **Anchor**, that is, apply the stimulus (e.g. pressing your thumb and index finger together), at the peak of the experience (see Diagram 10.1) and release after the peak.

5. **Change state.** Think about something neutral to clear your mind. This is known as "breaking state."

6. **Repeat steps 2 to 5 around four to six times.** If you want to anchor three states, I suggest that you use two examples of each of the three states, making six in total. If you want only one state, repeat the process four to six times with the same state, either choosing the same vivid experience (step 2) or different ones. Use the same anchor (e.g. thumb and index finger) each time; this is known as "stacking" anchors.

7. **Test** by "firing"/activating the anchor, for example, pressing your thumb and index finger together and noticing how you feel.

Tip 10.2

Do an interim test (step 7) after you have done two rounds of anchoring, so that if for some reason you are not doing the anchoring process correctly, you will be able to make changes earlier to save time rather than doing all six rounds.

A word about future pacing

If you have set a resource anchor for a specific event, such as a presentation to an important client, incorporate future pacing in step 7 (mentioned in Chapter 9, page 141, step 6). When you future pace the anchor, it is useful to do two types of visualizations. The first is *dissociated*, in other words, seeing yourself making the presentation as if on a TV or cinema screen. You fire your anchor and, at the same time, see yourself in the picture making the presentation with the resources you anchored. The second type is *associated*, in other words, imagining that you are in the situation as if looking through your own eyes, again with the anchor fired. With both types, you can do it with your eyes open or closed.

With dissociated visualization, you can often notice aspects of how you are behaving or performing, what you are doing, or not doing, to help the situation go well. Some people find one type more useful than the other. Find which type(s) work best for you.

An additional important point when future pacing is to consider several different scenarios, where in each scenario you are feeling the anchored state(s) and hence "performing" the way you want. The benefit of future-pacing different scenarios is that you can be prepared for almost all eventualities, not just preparing for things going perfectly (negotiators and audiences sometimes pose challenging questions). This will make you feel even more confident about the event. Therefore, do dissociated future pacing on several scenarios with your anchor fired (this typically takes between one and two minutes, as you will be able to speed up the situations in your mind) and then, a few seconds afterward, repeat it using associated future pacing for the same scenarios.

A final comment about anchoring yourself

If you have already created positive associations with certain visual, auditory, or kinesthetic stimuli, have access to them where possible. For example, have a picture of your children on your desk or screensaver, have certificates or pictures of medals on the wall of your office, have access to your favorite pieces of music (uplifting or calming) in case you need a boost before a meeting, or to calm down afterward! If you have a particular item of clothing that makes you feel special when you wear it, you can wear it for important meetings.

Exercise 10.1

(approx. 10–15 minutes for each type of anchor)

Using the previous anchoring process (seven steps to anchoring), and possibly supplemented by pictures or music, create two main types of anchor: an uplifting, positive one, and a relaxing, calming one.

Anchoring other people at work

As a manager, you can use the process explained in the previous sections to help a colleague set their own resource anchor.

You can also anchor people in other ways in the workplace. Remember, you can anchor using any or all of the representational systems.

You can anchor spatially. For example, when making a presentation, you can be in one spot when talking about the past, in another spot when talking about the present, and in another spot when you talk about the future (ideally these three spots would be to the left, center, and right of the stage as the audience looks at you). Having set up these three anchors spatially, you can either point to, or revisit, these spots as appropriate during the presentation to subtly indicate to the audience which time frame you are talking about.

Similarly, you could anchor certain states or responses spatially when presenting, for example, talking about an exciting event from one spot and about a negative event from a different spot. You can revisit each spot as appropriate during the presentation to "fire" the anchor (i.e. re-create the state) in the audience.

You can use stories and metaphors (Chapter 7) to help elicit and create a state in other people, for example, by telling an amusing story or an inspirational one. You can use gestures, words, or voice tonality to anchor others in meetings. For example, when selling, if the client/prospect talks about or shows a certain emotion or response, anchor it with a gesture. When relevant, you can fire the anchor (i.e. repeat the gesture) later.

Story 10.1

Several years ago, I was running a one-day sales training course. By this point, I was an experienced trainer, performing certain aspects of presentations automatically. At the start of the session, I made an amusing comment and the audience laughed, and as they were laughing I stepped forward slightly on one foot and made a small gesture. A few moments later, the audience were laughing about something, and I made the same movement and gesture. A minute or so later, I inadvertently made the same movement and gesture as I was talking about a *mildly* amusing situation and the audience started laughing. At that point, I realized fully how powerful anchoring can be with groups.

Exercise 10.2

(approx. 5–10 minutes)

Make a list of states that could be useful to anchor in other people in your role at work, for example, curiosity (e.g. about how competitors or customers will respond), excitement, and ready to take action. Pick one or two states and choose a way that you could subtly anchor it in others (a gesture, a word, a facial expression, tone of voice) and experiment with it in a suitable working situation.

Dealing with negative anchors at work

Just as there are positive anchors, sometimes negative anchors are created. For example, you might feel a little anxious when you hear a particular colleague's voice or when you go into a particular office because of a previous experience (again, this explanation is for a relatively minor negative situation). There is a specific NLP technique called "collapse anchors" which can be used with an individual and for which specialized NLP training is required. You can use the "collapse anchor" principles for yourself. Here is a brief summary of the process:

1. Set a positive, strong resource anchor and/or have a picture or hold a small object that creates a really strong positive state for you.

2. The next time you are in the situation when the negative anchor is activated, fire the strong positive anchor and keep doing so until the negative state disappears.

Story 10.2

One of my business-coaching clients felt anxious whenever he heard his boss approach his desk. I knew that he deeply loved his children and felt wonderful whenever he looked at their photo, remembering them saying, "I love you, Daddy." I suggested that the next time he heard his boss approaching, he hold and look at the picture and remember his children saying, "I love you, Daddy." He felt so good when this happened that it negated the previous negativity of his boss coming into the office, not just for that meeting but for all subsequent ones with him. This meant that he was able to deal with his boss in an appropriate way rather than based on a "pre-triggered" negative state.

Applications of anchoring at work

There are various applications of anchoring at work:

- **Presenting:** This includes preparing for the presentation, feeling resourceful during the presentation if there are difficult questions, and using spatial anchors. If you are speaking at a conference and there is a natural spot from where present-ers speak (at a specific table or by the lectern) and if the pre-vious speaker has in some way created a negative state in the audience (e.g. disappointment or boredom), then, if possible, present from a spot that is different from that of the previous speaker; when you see the audience to be in a good state, you can then move to the natural presenting spot. This acts as a "collapse anchor." You can also use a story or metaphor to help create this positive state in the audience.

- **Training:** As well as some of the items mentioned previously, you can use music as an anchor to let the group know that the exercise or break has finished. Also, if your courses are spread over modules, you can put the wall charts in the same place as for the previous module, so that delegates immediately feel fa-miliar with the training room.

- **Marketing and advertising:** The use of advertising jingles and corporate logos can act as a stimulus that leads to a response in customers. For example, many advertisements seek to create in customers feelings of being attractive and successful, and then link these feelings to their product, logo, and jingle.

- **Coaching/managing:** This includes helping clients and col-leagues to feel at their best in preparation for important meet-ings or interviews.

11

Seeing Other Perspectives

A key to understanding and insight

You have got to get along with people, but you also have to recognize that the strength of a team is different people with different perspectives and different personalities.
—Steve Case, co-founder and former CEO of AOL

By this point in the book, you will be very aware that each of us sees the world in our own unique way. One of the keys to success in business is being able to see situations from other perspectives, not just from your own. The NLP technique known as "perceptual positions" helps you to do this for yourself and also when seeking to influence others.

In which situations is "perceptual positions" useful?

For individuals, perceptual positions can be used to:

- Prepare for meetings, such as with colleagues, customers or prospects, suppliers and interviewers.
- Assist you to set goals (Chapter 4).
- Prevent and overcome conflicts or misunderstandings.
- Coach colleagues or individual clients to do the above.

Perceptual positions can be used on a more widespread or strategic level:

- Creative thinking, for example, designing consultancy solutions; according to Robert Dilts (one of the early NLP pioneers), Walt Disney used a form of perceptual positions to create his cartoon films.

- Strategic planning for departments, divisions, or whole organizations.

- Preparing for presentations to large groups.

Key concepts

Clichés such as "Put yourself in my shoes" and "There are three sides to every story: yours, mine, and the truth somewhere in between" give you an insight into the concepts of perceptual positions.

Most people have experienced being stuck in their own thinking at some time in their career. This is usually because the person is seeing a situation purely from their own point of view at that particular moment. In NLP, we call this being in *position 1* (or *first position*). The perspective of the other person(s) involved is called *position 2* (or *second position*); the perspective of the neutral observer is called *position 3* (or *third position*). The more easily you are able to detach yourself completely from position 1 and step into a "pure" position 2 and a "pure" position 3, the more effective you will be at using this invaluable technique.

On my training courses, I quite often hear delegates say that they can see other people's perspectives naturally, yet when they do the perceptual-positions exercise (explained in the following section), they discover that the technique is even more powerful and useful than they imagined. The reasons for this will be covered later.

The perceptual-positions process

Let's assume for illustrative purposes that you are using this process for yourself to gain some tips and insight into how to prepare for an important meeting with your boss. Examples of other uses of perceptual positions will be covered in the "applications" sections later in this chapter. As with the submodality and anchoring interventions in the previous two chapters, be clear about what you want from the exercise, how you would know that you have it, and that it is ecological to make the desired changes.

The process itself works as follows:

Step 1

Mark out three spaces (or use three chairs) on the floor in the shape of an equilateral or isosceles triangle (in a room where you won't be disturbed), rather as in Diagram 11.1. In this case, position 2 represents your boss, and position 3 represents a neutral observer.

Diagram 11.1

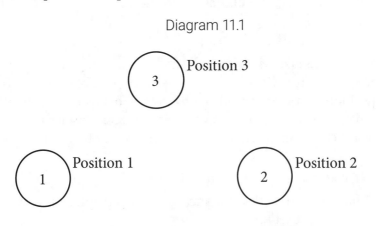

Step 2

Stand/sit in position 1, as yourself, looking at your boss in position 2, and ask yourself how you are feeling and what you are thinking as you face your boss. Typically spend no more than a minute there, enough time to become aware of your feelings about the situation.

Step 3

Go toward position 2, and when you are about halfway, break state by thinking of something completely unrelated in order to change your mindset from position 1 (break state was mentioned in step 5 of the seven-step anchoring process in Chapter 10). Then move to position 2, "becoming" your boss. As far as possible, adopt their physiology and posture, and "become" them (remember from the NLP Communication Model how physiology impacts on state and internal representations; see Tip 11.1 that follows). Spend as much time as you need (typically between two and five minutes) to gain insights into what your boss is thinking and feeling about the situation, as they look at "you" in position 1. Ask yourself questions such as:

- "What do I want from [name] in this meeting?"
- "What would you like to say to [name]?"
- "What information would I like from [name]?"
- "What else?"

Normally there are useful insights in position 2.

Step 4

When you have taken as many insights as you can, go towards position 3, and break state halfway as you did between positions 1 and 2. Then move to position 3, as an independent observer of (or advisor to) the situation, and adopt the posture that you would if you were considering a situation that you were not involved in. Ask yourself (as the observer) questions such as:

- "What advice would I give to both parties?"
- "What do I notice about the situation that perhaps those two people haven't yet noticed?"
- "What do they have in common/what are their common aims?"
- "If the person in position 1 did that (i.e. the behavior suggested in the answer to a previous question in position 3), what impact would it have on the person in position 2?" and vice versa.

Ask any other questions that are relevant to the specific scenario. It is important to be neutral and at the same time to realize that only the person in position 1 (i.e. you) can change as a direct result of this process. Make sure that position 3 is really detached from the other two positions, if necessary by making sure that position 3 is physically moved further away. Spend as much time as needed to gain insights about the situation.

Step 5

Take what you have learned from positions 2 and 3 and return to position 1 (i.e. you). What actions will you take and when? How has this new information informed your actions, preparations, etc.? Ask yourself to what extent you have achieved the outcomes you wanted from the exercise.

Step 6

In the unlikely event that you have not achieved as much as you wanted from this exercise, revisit one or more of the positions again, or even create a fourth position somewhere further back from the three positions in order to take an even more detached perspective. Remember always to finish at position 1, so that you can incorporate what you have learned.

Diagram 11.2 summarizes the process (the lines crossing the arrows represent a break state).

Diagram 11.2

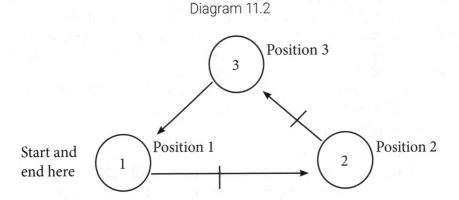

Tip 11.1

Please note that it is important to alter your physiology as mentioned previously, break state, "become" the person in position 2 (in this example, your boss), and "become" the neutral observer in position 3. The combination of moving to different locations and changing posture helps you to really identify with the different people and perceptual positions and consider it from *their* perspective, rather than doing it from *your* perspective of what they think. However, if it is not appropriate to move physically, for example, if this process is being done in a public place, you can do the process seated in chairs in conversation. It becomes even more important to break state between the three positions because there is no physical movement to a different spot.

Applications for individual use

Here are some examples where you can use perceptual positions at work in situations that are of a more individual nature. In all cases, position 3 is a neutral observer, and the process would be as outlined earlier. You could do it for yourself, or guide a colleague through the process, or ask the colleague to guide you through the process, once they have read and understood it. Please note that it is essential that the person acting as the guide follows the process, and resists any possible temptation to give opinions or ask leading questions. This process works best when the person being guided arrives at their own conclusions.

Applications include:

- **Selling, procurement, and negotiating:** You could use this before the meeting to get a better idea of what your prospects, clients, or suppliers could be looking for, or which negotiating stances they might take. Your client or supplier is represented in position 2. During the meeting itself, you might want to get into the mindset of position 2 or position 3. This would be one of those situations where you would use the perceptual positions process, or any relevant part of it, while remaining in *your* seat!

- **Interviewing:** Again, you could do this to help prepare for the meeting. Position 2 represents the person interviewing you or who you are interviewing.

- **Conflicts, misunderstandings, or dealing with "challenging" people:** You could do this to help you see someone else's perspective to help defuse a situation (not a major conflict or one where there are strong emotions attached; this is best done with the support of a qualified NLP professional). Please note that you would not do this in the presence of the person with whom you are in conflict; do it by yourself so that you can really see their point of view. Position 2 represents the other person in the situation. Consider asking a colleague to guide you through the process (having first read and understood the process); many NLP students say that having someone else asking the questions and having to verbalize the answers "forces" them to continue answering the questions in positions 2 and 3 and hence gain insights; it also "forces" them to commit to taking certain actions (step 5 of the process).

If you are acting in a coaching capacity, you could guide your "client" through the process for situations like those in the three preceding paragraphs.

Story 11.1

Simon, an NLP Practitioner, was the human resources director for a large publicly traded company. One of the directors was an extremely friendly man, who happened to be naturally tactile; unfortunately a young female member of staff perceived his natural manner as being sexual harassment and threatened to sue the company, which would have been a public relations disaster for them.

Simon spent 15–20 minutes taking the director through the perceptual-positions process as described earlier; the director really saw and felt how his behavior had impacted the young employee and felt sorry for his actions. Later that day Simon repeated the process with the young woman; she realized that the director was just being friendly and was like this with everyone and meant no harm.

The following day Simon spoke to both of them together; the director apologized and the employee dropped her complaint. We can only guess how much this process saved the company in terms of its reputation, legal fees, and associated time taken.

Applications for wider use

Here are some of the uses of perceptual positions where the situation involves more people or a larger group. We covered three main perceptual positions, but there is no limit to the number. In some of the examples that follow, there will be more than one position 2, such as if there are different groups within an audience. Please apply the principles to your own situation.

It is recognized that some of the following situations could be applied to individual situations such as those mentioned earlier, and vice versa:

- **Presentations to groups:** If the audience is homogeneous, then one position 2 will be sufficient. However, if there are some subgroups, I suggest that you create a separate position 2 (position 2a, 2b, etc.) when doing the exercise, with break states in between (for example, you might be presenting to an audience of professionals, in which case you might want to have a separate position for accountants, lawyers, surveyors, doctors, etc.). Sometimes it is helpful to have a specific person in mind to represent each of the groups during the exercise.

- **Strategic planning:** You could create several position 2s: customers, suppliers, competitors, employees, and shareholders. Position 3 could be an independent analyst in the City or Wall Street, or someone doing a consultative report into the position of your company within its market.

- **Departmental planning:** This would be broadly similar to the previous point, except that the position 2s would probably include other specific departments (marketing, finance, legal, etc.).

- **Product design, marketing:** In the early stages of product development, you could create different position 2s to represent the different target consumer groups.

- **Making important decisions:** You could create a separate position 2 for each of the main parties affected by the decision, then have position 3 as the independent consultant.

- **Creative solutions:** Walt Disney used a variation of the "perceptual positions" exercise when undertaking his creative-thinking processes. He would take his team into the "dreamer" room, to think of the wackiest ideas they could think of, the "critic" room to think of why all these ideas might not work, and the "realist" room to pull together the ideas from the other rooms.

- **Creative problem solving:** Position 1 represents the current situation, position 2 represents a time in the future when you have what you want or have solved the situation, and from position 3, you can observe how you got from the present to the future. From position 2, you can also give advice to yourself in the "past."

- **Using perceptual positions conversationally:** Perceptual positions can be used conversationally, with individuals or groups. For example, asking "If [name] were here now, what would he say?" or "If you were [name], how would you feel about this?" invites the person you are speaking with to go into position 2. Position 3 thinking can be similarly created by asking "If you were advising someone else about [this situation], what advice would you give them?"

Exercise 11.1

(approx. 15 minutes)

Think of a situation where it would be useful for you to have an insight into someone else's thinking about a topic. It does not need to be a major challenge, and you might find it useful to choose a relatively minor situation so that you can get used to the process. Do the "perceptual positions" exercise as explained in this chapter.

12

Changing the Meaning of Events

Turning negatives into positives and handling objections

In times of great stress or adversity, it's always best to keep busy, to plough your anger and your energy into something positive.

—Lee Iacocca, former president at Ford Motor Company and Chrysler

In Part III so far, we have covered four NLP techniques (Neurological Levels, submodalities, anchoring, and perceptual positions), which require a formal or semi-formal process to be followed. In this chapter, we will cover how to quickly change your thinking or that of other people about a work situation that appears negative using a selection of just a few simple questions or statements. In NLP, it is known as "reframing." Reframing is essentially making suggestions or statements with the intention of changing the interpretation of the situation.

In which situations is reframing useful?

Reframing is useful whenever you (or someone else) are thinking negatively about a situation. It is also the basis of handling objections in a sales context. Specific examples include selling, coaching, managing, presenting poor results, and negotiating.

Key concepts

By the very nature of the word "reframing," there is an implicit idea that there is already a "frame" around an event or situation. From the Communication Model, you will recognize that external events are filtered (i.e. deleted, generalized, and in particular, distorted) through a set of beliefs and experiences (i.e. a frame of reference) which leads to thoughts and feelings about the events.

Consequently, there are rarely events or situations that are inherently "bad"; events can be interpreted or explained in a variety of ways. Politicians and business leaders commenting on "bad news" are usually well versed in the art of "spin." For example, if a company announces annual profits that are lower than last year, many people will view that as a "disappointing" set of results. That is the frame or context through which it has been viewed. Reframing helps you and other people to explain or perceive the results in a more positive light. (Chapter 13 considers in greater depth different ways to change beliefs.)

You can reframe other people conversationally, and you can reframe yourself by changing the way you think.

Tip 12.1

Because events can be interpreted in many ways, as far as you reasonably can (without being delusional), interpret situations and events in ways that empower you the most.

The two main types of reframing

There are two main types of reframing:

- "Context" reframes.
- "Meaning" or "content" reframes.

Let's take each in turn.

Context reframe

A context reframe is where you consider the same specific behavior or event in a different context, such as a different time period or different situation, leading to a more positive assessment of the behavior or event. To do a context reframe, you ask yourself, "What/where/when would be a different context (or situation or place) where this behavior or event would be acceptable or even positive?" For example, someone's keenness to make sure that colleagues are happy at work might be seen as "fussing" or a nuisance, but if they were working in a customer-services role such as a waiter or air steward (i.e. a different situation or context), it would be a big advantage.

Examples of different contexts include different time periods (e.g. the future), different organizations you'll work for, or jobs you'll have in the future, and different cultures or locations.

Meaning (content) reframe

A meaning (or content) reframe is where you consider a different and more positive meaning of the same behavior. To do a meaning/content reframe, ask yourself, "What else could this behavior or event mean?" or "What's a more positive interpretation of the event?" For example, if a boss sometimes shouts at their team, it could be interpreted as being aggressive, which is negative, or it could be interpreted as being motivated and passionate, which is positive.

Tip 12.2

A useful way to do a meaning reframe is to change an important word. For example, if a customer says that your service is too expensive, you could reframe the word "expensive" and reply, "We offer a premium product at a price you would expect." I expand on this later in this chapter when covering how to handle objections (see page 174).

Practical tips for reframing

To repeat an earlier point, reframing is essentially making suggestions or statements with the intention of changing the interpretation of the situation. If the person you are speaking to does not take on board the different way of looking at the situation, there's no problem because, after all, you're just voicing a thought. That said, here are some important guidelines for reframing other people that will significantly increase the likelihood of their accepting your reframe.

Please ensure that:

1. You have permission (implicit or explicit) to reframe the person. For example, as a coach or trusted colleague, you would almost certainly have permission. If you are not sure, ask something like, "Is it okay if I offer you another perspective on this?" or "Are you okay to talk more about this?" I have coached clients who have been irritated by someone at work who was trying to put a positive spin on an event, almost certainly with the best of intentions, yet it was not the right time to do so or my client simply didn't want that particular person to do so.

2. The person is "open" to being reframed. Most people have had moments when they are upset or annoyed, and any further discussion at that moment would not be helpful.

3. You are in rapport with the other person. Sometimes reframes can appear flippant or humorous, so make sure that you are in rapport (Chapter 5).

4. The reframe is plausible. It does not have to be true, merely a plausible alternative view of the situation.

5. You say the reframe as if you believe it, particularly given point 3 above.

6. You have some knowledge of how the situation is a problem for the other person, so that you can choose a reframe that is appropriate for the other person based on their point of view rather than choose one from yours (this links to the NLP Presupposition of respecting other people's point of view; see Chapter 3). Where practical, ask the person how the situation is a problem for them.

7. Use common sense! Unless you are really skilled and qualified, reframing is best used for relatively minor situations.

Generally, a reframe would be worded as follows:

- "Well, at least you'll be able to...."
- "Isn't it great that she'll be able to...."
- "So now (at least/finally) you'll be able to...."

- "So at least you won't have to...."
- "Thank goodness you're not...."
- "Perhaps he hasn't/has/isn't/is/can't...."

Please note that reframing is *not* about giving advice. It is simply about asking the person to consider a different way of thinking about the event.

Here are some examples of reframing in business:

"I'm annoyed because my boss gives me more work than other members of the team."

Possible reframe 1: "Perhaps they think you're better able to cope than the other members of the team." (Meaning reframe—changes the interpretation of the behavior.)

Possible reframe 2: "Isn't it great that they trust you to get stuff done." (Meaning reframe.)

Possible reframe 3: "It may seem like a nuisance now, but when you go for your next promotion you'll be glad you had all this experience (won't you?)." (Context reframe—looking at a different time horizon.)

Possible reframe 4: "At least you've got a job!" (Meaning reframe.)

"It's so boring filling out all these job applications."

Possible reframe 1: "At least there are lots of possible jobs for you to go for." (Meaning reframe.)

Possible reframe 2: "Won't you be glad you did this when you've got the job you want?" (Context reframe.)

Possible reframe 3: "Doing this shows how committed you are to your own success and will stand you in good stead in your future career." (Meaning and context reframe.)

Exercise 12.1

Practice reframing. If you feel confident, do so with clients and colleagues. If you don't yet feel ready to reframe in "real life," you can practice as follows:

- Listen to interviews, read newspapers, or watch the news and, in your mind, put a positive spin on events.

- Find a willing partner. Ask the other person to tell you a relatively minor challenge they are facing and ask, "How is that a problem for you?" Once you have an idea of how it is a problem for the person, decide quickly on a couple of possible reframes and deliver the reframe. Using sensory acuity (Chapter 5), notice the impact of each reframe. Ask for feedback regarding how the reframes felt and how they could be improved.

Handling objections

The principles of reframing can be used to handle objections, for example, in a sales context. Here are some ways to do so, using the following two objections as examples:

1. "Your business has only been going for two years so you don't have enough experience for us."
2. "You're too expensive."

When reading the reframes that follow, remember that these are suggestions and that not all of them will be relevant in all situations. Remember to use common sense! Example response 1 refers to objection 1; example response 2 refers to objection 2.

Type: Redefine some of the key terms or concepts.

Example response 1: "It's because we are so new to this market that we can come up with innovative solutions with our fresh approach."

Example responses 2: "This is a premium price for a premium product," or "This is a long-term investment."

Type: Tell a metaphor or story.

Example response 1: "One of our existing clients loved the fresh approach and innovative solutions, and made a 20 percent efficiency improvement as a result."

Example response 2: "One of our clients saved more than the cost of our product in the first quarter."

Type: Give a counter-example.

Example response 1: "Microsoft was a young company once."

Example response 2: "Have you ever bought anything which seemed a little more than you wanted to pay but which proved to be a great investment?"

Type: Apply the objection to itself.

Example responses 1: "With your years of experience, I'm sure you've found examples of when young companies have provided excellent service," or "With your experience, you've probably found that experience can blind people to new alternatives."

Example response 2: "That could be a costly/expensive idea in the long run."

Type: Get specific.

Example response 1: "Exactly how long would you expect a business to be around before it's experienced enough for you?"

Example response 2: "Exactly how much more is this than you want to pay?" (Then deal with this smaller amount rather than the whole amount.)

Type: Link to something more important.

Example response 1: "Isn't it more important to have new, fresh, and leading ideas that will help you to...?" (Mention a value they have told you, such as being a market leader.)

Example response 2: "Isn't it more important to... than to concern yourself with a (relatively) small amount of money?"

Type: Think outside the box.

Example response 1: "Although the company may be new, the three lead consultants have 30 years' experience between them."

Example response 2: "In five years' time, you'll see this investment as money well spent."

This topic is explored in more detail in Robert Dilts' book *Sleight of Mouth: The Magic of Conversational Belief Change.*

Applications for individual use

You can reframe yourself, or your colleagues, in the following types of situation:

- **Stimulating clients'/colleagues' thinking:** Examples include where they do not know what to do next, or can see only a small number of alternatives, in which case reframing can help them think outside the box.

- **Managing staff:** To help provide a rationale for taking a particular course of action.

- **Turning disappointments into opportunities:** Examples include not winning a sale, not being successful at a job interview, and not getting a promotion.

- **Overcoming challenges:** Examples include responding to other people's inefficiency or apparent intransigence, and meeting deadlines.

- **Making unpleasant tasks seem more pleasant:** Doing routine work such as filing; difficult conversations with colleagues or customers.

- **Handling objections:** For example, when selling or persuading colleagues about your ideas.

Applications for wider use

You can also reframe in these situations:

- **Handling objections when presenting to groups:** Examples include pitching for large-scale contracts and answering questions from attendees/delegates at a training seminar.

- **Training staff to handle customer queries:** Customer-facing staff can be taught how to reframe.

- **Press releases:** If there is some "bad news," such as poor profit figures, you can use the principles of reframing to paint the situation in the most positive way.

13

Changing Beliefs

Simple and powerful ways to alter your thinking

Whether you think that you can, or that you can't, you are usually right.
—Henry Ford, founder of the Ford Motor Company

As you know, beliefs are a key filter creating your internal reality. There are many belief-change techniques in NLP. In this chapter, we will build on the reframing work from the previous chapter and cover how to change beliefs conversationally.

Why is belief change so useful?

Given that beliefs play such a powerful role in defining your results, being able to change your own negative or limiting beliefs (or those of others) can help to:

- Improve work results.
- Coach or manage others to improve their results.
- Enable you or others to fulfil potential at work.

Key concepts

Beliefs can be defined as "our best current thinking about a topic" or "those convictions that we hold as being true." When someone else has a belief, we usually refer to it as "an opinion," yet when we have a belief, we tend to call it "the truth."

Beliefs therefore can be positive and empowering, or limiting and disempowering. If you have an empowering belief (e.g. "I am a good salesperson/manager/designer," or "I can learn new skills easily"), then keep it! If you have a limiting belief (e.g. the opposite of the empowering beliefs mentioned previously), then this chapter will show you some ways to change it. Please note that limiting beliefs that have a major negative consequence are outside the scope of this book and are best addressed by NLP Practitioners, coaches, or (in more extreme cases) counselors with suitable training.

A limiting belief is one that will in some way limit you from being, doing, or having what you want to be, do, or have. Such beliefs could be about:

- You or your capabilities: "I am not able to sell," or "I don't come across well at interviews."

- Other people: "You can't trust accountants," or "All bosses treat staff badly."

- The world at large: "People are selfish," or "Life always kicks you when you're down."

Here are some tips to help you to identify limiting beliefs.

1. "Feelings" that you can't actually feel (because it's not an emotion) and where you could replace the word "feel" with "believe," such as "I feel people don't like me" or "I feel I need to worry before a presentation."

2. Negations, such as "I'm not able to learn new things," or "I can't have a successful career."

3. Comparisons, such as "I can't make enough money," or "I'm not clever enough."

4. "Necessity" words (have to, got to, should, must, need to), such as "I have to know all the answers" or "I should phone all my customers, even the unprofitable ones."

Exercise 13.1

(approx. 2–10 minutes)

Make a list of any key limiting beliefs that you have which limit your career or business progress. Pick one at a time and go through the next section with this belief in mind with the intention of changing the belief.

Please be mindful of the difference between a limiting belief (future implications) and a statement of fact (past or present based). It may be true that your colleague has never done a presentation; it's a limiting belief that they can't become good at presenting.

Tip 13.1

Please also bear in mind the Neurological Levels model (Chapter 8) and the link between confidence (i.e. belief) and competence (i.e. capabilities). Believing that you can do something that you cannot is probably stupid or even dangerous. Would you want your tax affairs managed by a confident person who knows nothing about taxation?

Changing beliefs conversationally

Here are some ways to reduce the impact of (or even to remove completely) minor limiting beliefs, either yours or those of your colleagues. Not all of these will be relevant for every belief.

Look for counter-examples (Chapter 12, Handling objections).

Ask yourself, "Where or when has this belief not been true (either for me or for other people)?" One of my clients believed that she couldn't present well to groups. I challenged her and she was then able to name several situations where she had presented effectively to groups, which led to her changing her belief.

Use perceptual positions (Chapter 11). Often putting yourself in someone else's shoes (position 2), or imagining it as a neutral observer (position 3), will change how you perceive the situation. For example, I asked a financial-advisor client, faced with a belief that he didn't know how to expand his business, what advice he would give someone else in the same situation (position 3). After a pause, he made several really useful suggestions.

Use reframing (Chapter 12). Look for the positive elements in the situation. How could this situation be useful to you? What are the positives from this?

Check your reality. Sometimes we make assumptions and then start believing them. It could be worth asking yourself, "How do I know this belief is true?" or even "How do I know this belief isn't false?"

Increase your capabilities. If we think back to Chapter 8 and the Neurological Levels alignment, limiting beliefs may result from lack of skills. Using the example of the presenter above, even if she were not able to do effective presentations, learning additional presentation skills would probably have helped her.

Pretend: Ask yourself, "What would someone who could do this do? How would they act?" and then do that. Fake it until you make it! One of the principles of NLP is to model excellence by replicating the behaviors of someone who is excellent.

Model yourself: Ask yourself where or when you have been faced with a similar challenge (possibly in a different context) that you successfully dealt with? How did you do that? Which strategies, states, and attitudes could you replicate in this situation? For example, you might believe that you are not good at making presentations at work, yet you gave a great speech as the best man at your friend's wedding. How did you do that?

Use the "mindset for success": Revisit the positive beliefs and the Principles for Success (Chapter 3). Behave as if these were true. Remember to be *At Cause*.

Use your resource anchor: One of my clients was about to attend an interview for a job that she (and many other candidates) really wanted and about which she was really nervous. She believed that the interviewers would ask her questions that she wouldn't be able to answer. She used her resource anchor (Chapter 10) and was able to handle all the questions appropriately even when she didn't know the answer; she got the job!

What's your purpose? Refer to some of the goal-setting questions (Chapter 4). Sometimes, getting in touch with your values, sense of identity, or purpose (Chapter 8) will help you find the motivation to overcome a limiting belief. Remember, the higher Neurological Levels tend to be more powerful than the lower ones.

You have changed beliefs before. You have probably believed at some time that you couldn't do something, yet found later that you could. Think now of several times when you have done this, for example, unexpectedly won a large contract or got promoted. Could the current limiting belief simply be another example of a belief that you will realize in the future was not true?

Applications for individual use

You can change your own limiting beliefs, or help individual colleagues and clients do so, in almost every area of work, for example, sales, presentations, or going for a new job.

Applications for wider use

You can use these principles with groups, for example, to help motivate staff after bad financial results or to increase self-belief in a group when running a training course.

Part IV

Understanding, Influencing, and Motivating

People at Work

Part IV looks at two particularly important filters and aspects of personality, namely, values and meta programs.

Chapter 14 looks at values (also known as criteria) in more depth and describes how to find out what is important to someone and how useful this is in organizations.

Chapter 15 describes personality traits known in NLP as "meta programs." These are deep filters that can help you to understand, predict, and influence behavior.

14

Values

The key to motivating and influencing

---

*Motivation is the art of getting people to do what
you want them to do because they want to do it.*
—Dwight D. Eisenhower, former U.S. President

We referred to values in the Communication Model (Chapter 2) and in the Neurological Levels model (Chapter 8). Values can be defined as the things that we want, look for, or which are important to us in any given context. They are one of the most important filters and an awareness of values will be useful for you personally in your own working life as well as for enhancing your ability to influence other people at work.

Why is a knowledge of values so important?

Values will help you to:

- Sell more.
- Manage so effectively that you will have staff clamoring to work for you.
- Improve your own satisfaction level at work.
- Make better decisions and choices about your career.
- Negotiate more effectively.
- Recruit better staff.
- Prevent or minimize the sources of conflict at work.
- Build more effective teams.
- Coach other people, including in the previous topics.

Key concepts

Values are usually intangible and, from a Hierarchy of Ideas perspective (Chapter 7), an abstract concept. Examples of values in the workplace for an individual could be *challenge, respect, variety,* and *making a difference* and, for an organization, *service, excellence, innovation,* and *empowerment.* Because values are intangible, they might mean different things to different people; *your* definition of, for example, *variety* might be different from that of one of your colleagues.

You might also hear the term "criteria" used by NLP professionals when referring to values; essentially the terms are interchangeable.

Values are those things that we either move toward having, or move away from not having. For example, money might be important to one of your colleagues because they want what money can buy (house, car, clothes, etc.) and it might be equally as important to another colleague because they do not want to be without money and have the sparse home life they had when growing up. The first colleague is motivated by moving toward money, and the second is motivated by the thought of not having it (known as moving away from). This will be discussed further in the next chapter.

Values link to beliefs, attitudes, and behaviors. Sometimes a person's values are formed because of a belief they have; sometimes beliefs are formed because of a value they have. A manager may value honesty, because they believe that it is important to tell the truth. Their attitudes, which are essentially beliefs and values around a specific topic, will reflect this, and assuming they are congruent (see alignment and congruence in Chapter 8), their behavior will reflect their beliefs, values, and attitudes.

Values are naturally organized in a hierarchy. There will be several things that are important to you at work or in your career or business; some of these will be more important than others. As we will soon cover, this becomes really important when working with values. Values can and do change throughout a person's life and career, especially when a significant event happens, such as being laid off, being promoted, or becoming a parent.

In the context of motivation at work, there are numerous theories. One that is particularly relevant is by Frederick Herzberg, who found that there are two main types of motivator at work—"hygiene factors" (such as work conditions, status, salary, and company car) and "true motivators" (such as recognition, advancement, the work itself, and responsibility). For more information on theories about values, see the "Resources for Further Learning" section.

Working with values

There are many ways to use values in the workplace. The starting point when working with values is to find out, or elicit, someone's values in the relevant context. For example, if you are managing or acting as a coach for someone around a career choice, the context is "career"; if you are selling them a car, the context is "car."

The process of eliciting values when you have the "client's" overt permission is described in the following section (later in the chapter we will cover how to elicit values more informally when you might not have overt permission). Let's assume that you have been asked by a colleague to help them with their next career move; the context therefore is "career."

Step 1: Standard questions

Ask your colleague, "What's important to you in/about a career?" or "What do you look for in a career?" or "What do you want from a career?" All of these questions are similar, and I usually ask all three together because clients and students have said that they find it useful.

Write down the answers using your colleague's words (*not* your paraphrased version). The word or phrase that they say will mean something specific to them, and this is about them, **not** you. If the value that they give is stated in the negative, for example, "not being ignored," ask, "What do you want instead?" to get a value stated in the positive (e.g. "recognition"), which is what you would write down. If there is a slightly extended pause (as a guide, there is often a pause after the first four to seven values), ask, "What else is important to you about your career?" Keep going until the colleague seems to have run out of ideas.

Tip 14.1

Keep quiet while your colleague is reflecting on their values and resist any temptation to suggest values, as this process is about *their* values, not yours.

Step 2: Previous situations

Because having your values met will usually make you happy and motivated, an additional way to find out your colleague's values is to ask them to remember a specific time when they felt really motivated or happy in their career, and what was it about that time that led them to feel so happy or motivated. As they describe the situation, listen out for values. It is likely that they will mention some of the values that they mentioned in step 1. If there is a value that they didn't mention previously in step 1, ask them if that is important to them in their career. Assuming that it is, add it to the list. If you are hearing several values that were not mentioned in step 1, repeat step 2 with a different situation to elicit additional values.

At this stage, you will probably have between 8 and 12 values. If it is slightly more or slightly less, then that's fine. Occasionally people will give a lot more than 12, which indicates either that some of the values could be grouped together, for example, *honesty, trust,* and *integrity* could be similar for a particular person, or that the values are in fact "behaviors." As a guide, values are intangible, whereas behaviors are tangible. If your colleague mentions a behavior, ask, "What's important to you about that?" which will lead to their giving you the related value.

Step 3: "Catch-all"

Show them the list of values and ask, "If you had all of this (these values) in your career, would you want it or is there anything missing?" which will identify any values not previously mentioned. Occasionally the person might say that there is something missing, in which case add it to the list and repeat the question until there is nothing else that they want to add.

Tip 14.2

Sometimes in steps 1, 2, or 3, people will want to explain why each value is important. Though this will be useful later, it is not useful at this point. If your colleague explains or gives long-winded answers, politely and graciously suggest that the best way for them to get the benefit from this process is to give a brief answer regarding what is important to them in their career, and that there's no need to explain or justify the values.

Step 4: Ranking

Although all of the values on the list will be important to your colleague, some will be more important than others. Ask them to rank the values from 1 to 8, with 1 being the most important. Typically the top four to six values will provide the major amount of motivation in any given context.

Another way of ranking, especially if there are more than 10 values, is to rank the essential values as "As," the important but not essential values as "Bs" and the "icing on the cake" values as "Cs." I always ask my clients which method they would prefer or which would be most useful to them given the purpose of the exercise. Most people prefer the second method ("As," "Bs," and "Cs").

It is not uncommon for people to mention some of the more important values toward the end of the process. This indicates that the person has been searching deeper inside him or herself and emphasizes the importance of allowing the person time to think quietly, and of asking, "What else is important to you?" and doing steps 2 and 3.

Tip 14.3

When eliciting and ranking values, it is sometimes helpful to people to:

- Read out the values mentioned during the process. This might be particularly helpful to people whose preferred representational system is auditory.
- Sit next to the person so that they can see what you have written (for people with a visual preference).
- Let the person write the rankings next to each value (step 4) (for people with a kinesthetic preference).
- Rewrite the list, or let the person do it if they want to, once the person has ranked the list.

Step 5: Check

As a "check," offer them two careers: one with values 5 to 8 (name them) (or the "Bs" and "Cs") and the second with values 1 to 4 (name them) (or the "As"). I would expect them to choose the second one. If they were unsure or chose the first one, revisit step 4 and ask them to adjust the ranking.

Exercise 14.1

(approx. 10–20 minutes)

Choose the most appropriate word to reflect the context of work for you (e.g. career, or work, or business, or job) and do the values-elicitation exercise (steps 1–5) for that area so that you can gain greater insight or clarity. If you would find it easier, ask a trusted colleague or friend to take you through the process, bearing in mind the whole process and the tips.

Exercise 14.2

(approx. 10–20 minutes)

If you believe that it would be important to you in your work role to be able to elicit other people's values (if you sell, recruit, or manage people, it will be essential), practice the values-elicitation process with willing colleagues or friends.

Delving deeper: Criteria equivalents

As I mentioned earlier, because values are abstract, they will mean different things to different people. Therefore, it can be extremely useful (for reasons that I will explain further in the "applications" sections) to know what the person means by their stated values, and how specifically they would know whether their values had been met (or not). The term "criteria equivalent" is used in NLP to describe this.

Here is a selection of questions you could ask to find out what each of the values means. Let's assume that one of your colleague's work values is "recognition." Normally you would ask just one or two of these questions for each value (select the question(s) that are most appropriate).

- What has to happen for you to know that you are being recognized/have recognition at work?
- How do you know when you're being recognized at work?
- What does recognition mean to you at work?
- How do you know when someone (or something) recognizes you at work?
- What is your evidence procedure for recognition at work?
- What causes you to feel recognized at work?
- What would have to happen for you to feel not recognized at work or that your value of recognition was not being met?

Once you have steps 1–5 above, if it were appropriate, you would then find the criteria equivalents for the top few values, normally the top five, or all the "As," and for even more values if you think it would be useful. Using the example of your colleague, it will almost certainly be important to them to know both the values and the criteria equivalents, so that they can make a better choice of career.

Typically, finding the criteria equivalents takes 2–5 minutes per value, depending on how much detail is required. Therefore, within around 45 minutes, you will know a huge amount about them and/or have helped them gain that knowledge about him or herself.

Exercise 14.3

(approx. 20–45 minutes)

Continue Exercises 14.1 and 14.2, eliciting the criteria equivalents for the top few values. Do as many as you (14.1) or the colleague (14.2) would find useful.

Tip 14.4

Please note that values can and do change over time. I suggest that you revisit your career values periodically, perhaps before your annual appraisal or whenever there is a significant change in your work or personal circumstances. Also, if a few days after doing the values-elicitation exercise you realize that you have not listed an important value, simply add it to the list.

Applications for individual use

There are numerous ways you can use values at work for yourself or other individuals.

Making choices

As with the example we used in this chapter, you can help yourself or another person choose a new job or career. Elicit the values and criteria equivalents, then make a list of the alternatives and note whether each individual value is met in each of the choices. The table below gives an example.

Table 14.1

Value (listed in order of importance)	Career D	Option E	Option F
Challenge	√	√	√
Variety	√	?	√
Making a Difference	X	X	√
Recognition	√	X	√
Development	?	√	√

Assuming that the five values are all "As," then Option F "ticks all the boxes"! You might prefer to use scores out of 10 for each value rather than ticks, Xs, and question marks.

Job interviews (as a candidate)

If you know your values, hierarchy/ranking, and criteria equivalents, you will be able to ask the interviewer(s) searching questions regarding the role to find out whether it is truly suitable for you. Whenever I cover values on my training courses, I ask the attendees (most of whom have staff reporting to them) what they would think about a candidate who asked searching and relevant questions about the role. The response is **always** that they would think highly of the candidate, which increases the candidate's chances of success.

Improving your satisfaction at work

Using the principles detailed in "Making choices" in this section, list your values in order of importance and then score on a scale of 1 to 10 the degree to which each value is being met in your current role. Depending on the situation, it might be appropriate to make specific requests to your boss regarding how to improve your level of satisfaction.

Selling to consumers

When you bought the shoes you're wearing, you had an idea of what you wanted in a pair of shoes (style, size, price, color etc.), that is, your values or criteria. A good salesperson would have asked you what you want in a pair of shoes and then showed you shoes that fit your criteria (see Story 14.1). This "informal" values elicitation process uses the same principles as the more "formal" process we covered earlier in this chapter.

Goal setting

As discussed in Chapter 4 and Chapter 8, when setting goals, you need to make sure that you know your values and that your values are in alignment with your goals. In other words, will achieving your goal give you more of your essential values, or the top three or four values?

Story 14.1

Although asking customers what they are looking for may seem very obvious, when I cover the application of values to selling in a course, every person admits that they have had experiences of salespeople not doing even a basic values elicitation. A few years ago, Alison, a course attendee who had learned about values in a previous module, was looking for a brand-new, top-of-the-range car. She described walking into one car dealership and being approached by a salesman who proceeded to tell her about the various cars that were available. Amused, and slightly surprised, she listened for around five to 10 ten minutes, hoping that he would actually ask her what she wanted in a car. He did not and, needless to say, she went to a different showroom.

Coaching individuals

You could coach individuals in the areas listed previously if you are their manager or hired as a business coach.

Applications within organizations

There are numerous applications of values for organizations.

Managing and motivating staff

This is a really important use of values and an invaluable way for managers to create or enhance employee engagement. I suggest that every manager be trained to do the following two-step process.

Step 1: Do a values-elicitation exercise with each employee at their annual appraisal, which will take up to one hour, including the criteria equivalents. Set the scene by saying something along the lines of:

As your boss, it's really important to me that you're happy and motivated in your work. Why? Because you'll produce better results, which will benefit you, me, the team, and our customers/clients/ patients. I consider it my role to help you to be as happy in your work as possible and to help you to have as much of what you want at work and as little of what you don't want. I promise you I will do everything in my power to do this, subject to the various budgetary and organizational limits that exist. And remember, I am not a mind-reader, so if you don't tell me what's important to you, I can't be expected to know. So, on the basis that I'm not a mind-reader and that I promise to do my best for you, would you be willing to answer a few questions?

I've never heard of an employee reply "no." You would then proceed into steps 1–5 and find the criteria equivalents.

Tip 14.5

A couple of weeks before the annual appraisal, ask your employees to think about what's important to them in their job/ work/career. This gives them the chance to reflect before the appraisal.

Step 2: Keep your word. If circumstances change during the year, explain that to the employees affected.

Tip 14.6

Be curious regarding the degree to which your staff 's values link to Herzberg's true motivators (as discussed earlier in this chapter). Even in a challenging economic environment, where there might be less scope to use money to motivate staff, there are still ways to get the best from people if you understand what truly motivates them.

Story 14.2

I teach this process on *every* management-related course that I run. Without exception, all attendees confirm that if their boss did this process, including keeping their word, they would feel highly motivated and want to work for that boss.

Making choices regarding suppliers or expensive items

As with the "Making choices" section earlier, do a full values elicitation and evaluate according to the list.

Selling to businesses

The approach is similar to the one outlined under "Selling to consumers" previously. If you are selling a larger-scale item to a business, you will probably be having a longer conversation or series of conversations with the prospect. During that time, listen for when the prospect mentions values relating to the product. Because values are important, often you will be able to use sensory acuity to notice a shift in posture or voice tonality as the prospect mentions the word or phrase. You might also be able to do a values elicitation similar to the way we described earlier in this chapter. The scene-setting may go something like this (assume that you are selling consultancy services):

I find that most of my clients want to be more [value previously mentioned or that is bound to be important, such as profitable/ efficient/successful]. I assume that's something that you're interested in. In order that I can help you to become more [value], is it okay to ask you some questions?

Assuming they say "yes," elicit their values according to steps 1–5 and then elicit the criteria equivalents. You would probably adjust the questions slightly, given that it is a formal business situation. For example, you would replace "career" with "consultancy provider" or "consultancy services" in step 1 and, when ranking (step 4), you would probably ask for the most important three or four values, or the really essential ones.

Once you know what's really important to them in a firm of consultancy providers and what they mean by each of the values (i.e. the criteria equivalents), your role as a salesperson becomes relatively straightforward; demonstrate how your service fits their needs. By selling in this way, you are really serving your client.

Tip 14.7

Occasionally people find selling uncomfortable. When they realize that this process helps them to truly serve customers/ clients (a win–win approach), their attitude to selling becomes far more positive and enthusiastic.

Relationship management

The approach would be similar to "Selling to businesses," that is, eliciting the client's values around what they want from your company or from the relationship.

Negotiation

Though there are many aspects to successful negotiating, it is really useful if you can find out what is important and not important to your counter-party. Use your sensory acuity as mentioned in "Selling to businesses" to recognize values.

Recruitment

Do a values elicitation for the role, that is, decide which values you want in a candidate, and interview against that list, using an approach similar to "Making choices." Also, elicit the values and criteria equivalents for the candidates' career/work/job to get a sense of whether they are suited to the role.

Team building

Though this is not the only way to build an effective team, asking each team member to explain their values and equivalents to their colleagues normally leads to a greater understanding and empathy. If you are leading the team, please think carefully before doing this exercise. It normally works well with a team that is functioning well, but might not be suitable if the team has "baggage."

Organizational culture change

This was covered in the Neurological Levels section (Chapter 8). It is important that the senior management and directors "walk their talk." If, for example, "approachability" is one of the stated business values, it is essential that this applies throughout the organization—starting from the top.

Conflicts

Often conflicts are caused because there is a clash of values, or because one party disregards (deliberately or accidentally) the values of the other party. By understanding the respective values of both parties and, if appropriate, bringing them to each other's awareness, negotiators and mediators can work to resolve the conflict.

15

Meta Programs

A deeper understanding of how to influence people at work

To effectively communicate, we must realize that we are all different in the way we perceive the world and use this understanding as a guide to our communication with others.
—Tony Robbins, author and coach

The final set of filters we will be covering is "meta programs." These are deep filters that, along with values and beliefs, greatly influence and shape our personality and responses to situations at work. They influence how we think about situations, almost regardless of the specific events that are happening. They are like "frames of mind." You might have found that you have said the same thing to two people at work and got very different responses, or said something to a colleague or customer and got a response that was completely unexpected. This is probably due to their respective meta-program patterns.

Why are meta programs so useful?

Having an awareness and understanding of meta programs will give you a greater understanding of yourself and other people, and help you to communicate your ideas and influence more effectively in business.

Every person you will ever meet at work will be running a series of meta programs. Having an understanding of these will help you to understand and influence their behavior in numerous work situations, including:

- Managing staff.
- Recruitment and selection.

- Selling.
- Negotiating.
- Presenting information.
- Coaching.
- Advertising.
- Team building, to ensure that you have an appropriate mix of people.
- General communication with colleagues.

At an extreme, an understanding of meta programs can prevent you or others from getting angry and having arguments (see Story 15.1, page 205).

Meta programs are easy and quick to use and, unlike most other methods of personality assessment, you can do this conversationally and quickly. Indeed, someone familiar with this information can elicit someone else's meta programs in 10–15 minutes.

Key concepts and background

Meta programs are patterns of thinking and responding that can be likened to "frames of mind." These frames of mind could be thought of as patterns or "programs" that lie above and beyond (i.e. "meta") the actual words or content of the situation; hence the term "meta programs." These meta programs will probably change when the context changes. For example, your responses to a situation when you are managing someone might be different from those in a similar situation when you are meeting clients, and they will almost certainly be different from how you respond at home or with friends. Therefore, your meta programs in any given context will determine your perspective, your way of thinking and feeling about situations, and hence your behaviors and responses.

Meta programs link to a well-known personality-profiling system called the Myers–Briggs Type Indicator (MBTI). You might have heard of this; I will not be expanding on it in this book, because much has already been written about it in many books and on the Internet (*Please Understand Me* by Keirsey and Bates provides an excellent explanation of MBTI). In some schools of NLP, the four MBTI traits (introvert–extrovert, sensor–intuitor, thinker–feeler, judger–perceiver) are referred to as "simple" meta programs, with the traditional NLP meta programs being referred to as "complex" meta programs. Many of the meta programs are a spectrum, where there are two extremes and two or three stages between the extremes.

For each of the meta programs, there is a question that you can ask to elicit the person's preference. Having asked the question, by listening carefully to the reply, you can make an excellent "guess" at someone's meta-program profile, then "test" it subsequently. Shelle Rose Charvet, well known for her use of meta programs (covered in her book, *Words That Change Minds*), often refers to the "guess and test" method. One way to "test" whether your guess is accurate is to use language and statements that are relevant to your guess and then watch the other person's response. All of this will be explained in the next section.

The meta programs and how to use them

Although there are variations in the number of meta-program filters taught, depending on which school of NLP you attend and which book you read (for example, *Figuring Out People* by L. Michael Hall and Bob Bodenhamer describes 51 meta programs), we will cover 15 filters that are widely taught and applicable at work. We will take each in turn and provide, where applicable:

- The name of the meta-program filter.
- A brief overview.
- The extremes of the spectrum of the filter (if applicable), with a description of the respective personality traits and indications of mid-ground if relevant. For some meta programs, there are categories rather than a spectrum.
- The question(s) you can ask to identify the meta-program preference.
- How to interpret the response and form your estimate of where the person is along the spectrum.
- The types of language to use to influence the person; please use an appropriate mix, depending on where the person is along the spectrum.
- Any relevant tips or pointers (*Words That Change Minds* quotes some research into the distribution of the meta-program traits in the workplace). Where the distribution is not fairly evenly

spread across the spectrum according to the research, I will mention this and how to apply it.

Please note that although the terminology used for the meta programs might vary from book to book, the principles will be similar. Also, the labels of the meta programs or the extremes of the spectrum might have slightly different meanings from how the word would be used in everyday language.

It is essential to realize that there are no inherently good, or bad, meta-program profiles; all traits can be useful or not useful, depending on the situation. The key is to be able to know your own traits, recognize those of other people, and be able to respond accordingly. This links to two of the NLP Presuppositions: "respect other people's opinion and individuality" and "be flexible" (the latter also being one of the Principles for Success).

How to get the most from this chapter

This is the longest chapter in this book. I have endeavored to find a balance between thoroughness and brevity. Several books have been written on the subject of meta programs alone; there are training courses lasting several days teaching this subject. Ultimately, it is up to you, the reader, to decide to what extent and how quickly you want to use the information in this chapter. My suggestion would be to use it initially to gain a better understanding of your own personality traits and those of other people important to your work performance. Once you have grasped that, you can start to deliberately elicit this information from others and use the relevant influencing language where appropriate.

Tip 15.1

As you read through these meta-program traits, see whether you can identify where you are on each spectrum at work, and where important clients or colleagues are.

Please note that the terms "meta programs," "filters," and "patterns" are often used interchangeably in this chapter because you might hear NLP Practitioners use these terms interchangeably. Throughout this chapter, the term "colleague" will be used when referring to the person exhibiting the various meta-program traits.

1. Values

Overview: This is often considered to be one of the meta programs and is certainly important for the next filter we'll be covering. We covered values in detail in the last chapter. If you are specifically using values in the contexts referred to in the last chapter, then elicit values in the ways described previously. If you are eliciting values purely as a way to elicit the next meta program, you won't need to go into as much detail as described in Chapter 14.

Questions to ask: "What's important to you about [context]? Anything else?"

Interpreting the response: This has been covered in Chapter 14. Simply recognize that the values are important to the colleague.

Examples of influencing language: Use the words that the colleague has used. Because values are important motivators, they will be motivated at the prospect of having their values met.

2. Direction filter

Overview: How do you keep motivated? Are you focused on an objective/goal, or on a situation or thing to be avoided?

The spectrum: "Toward" and "away from."

- "Toward" colleagues want to have, achieve, or get something they want. They tend to be good at prioritizing and setting and achieving goals. They might not spot problems because they are so focused on their goal or target.

- "Away from" colleagues, at the other end of the spectrum, do something to avoid certain events, situations, or things. They tend to be good at, and motivated by, spotting and preventing problems. They might not be good at prioritizing or achieving, because they will be distracted if something is wrong or not to their liking. Their results at work may be inconsistent (or achieved with inconsistent levels of effort—see Story 15.1, page 205) because once they have moved away from being uncomfortable they lose motivation.

- Colleagues can also be "mainly toward," "equally toward and away from," or "mainly away from," representing where the colleague is along the spectrum.

Question(s) to ask:

- "Why is [value] important to you in the context of [context]?"
- "And why is **that** [or repeat the key points from the previous answer] important to you?"
- "And why is **that** [or repeat the key points from the previous answer] important to you?"

In other words, you ask the same question three times, to drill down into the reply. If you were being really thorough, you would do this for all values. In practice, and to save time, for the first question, ask, "Why are all these (values) important to you?" so that you only go through the three questions once.

Interpreting the response: Colleagues with a "toward" pattern will use words such as "get," "have," "obtain," "reach," "earn," or "win," or similar ideas. Colleagues with an "away from" pattern will mention what they don't want to happen, situations to avoid or get rid of, or use negations. They might mention words indicating necessity like "have to," "must," "should," and "ought to." You can estimate where the colleague is along the spectrum by the proportion of "toward" and "away from" responses given.

Examples of influencing language:

- Toward: This is what you will gain/achieve/win/earn; targets; target date; objectives; goals.
- Away from: Mention situations to be avoided or problems to be solved; deadline; get rid of; exclude; reduce problems and liabilities.

Use an appropriate mixture, depending on where the colleague is along the spectrum. (This applies to all the meta programs to follow.)

Tips:

- When speaking to a mixed audience, or writing a report where you don't know the reader, use a combination of "toward" and "away from" language to ensure that you reach all of the audience and avoid turning off some of the audience. Did you notice both patterns in the previous sentence ("reach" and "avoid turning off")?

- Some products are more likely to be at one end of the spectrum. For example, health insurance is generally an "away from" product, whereas luxury jewelry is probably a "toward" product.

Story 15.1

Not long after I had learned about meta programs, I was part of a team doing a project using NLP modeling skills (see Chapter 16) to identify the traits of successful salespeople at a large multinational company. Each team member was given a number of people, some of whom were performing excellently and some performing not so well, and we weren't told who was in which category. I interviewed one man who told me he was always near the top of the sales league. I assumed that he was a "toward" person so that when he asked why he was being interviewed, I used very "toward" language such as "the company wants to recruit great salespeople to expand on its success." The salesman said, "I don't understand this, and I feel so angry that I could hit you." I was slightly taken aback, and then I remembered that he had said that he works 20–30 hours a week in the first part of the month, and then as deadlines and targets loom, he works 80–90 hours per week (i.e. an "away from" pattern). Recognizing the "away from" pattern, I then said, "Think how bad it would be for you and other people if the company employed salespeople who weren't up to the job. You wouldn't want that, would you?" He replied, "Oh, now I understand. Sorry for being a bit irritable earlier."

---

3. Reason filter

Overview: how do you approach your daily work? Do you strive for new/other ways to do it, or do you prefer to follow established procedures?

The spectrum: "Options" and "procedures."

- "Options" colleagues prefer to strive for new or other ways to do their work. They resist following established procedures, preferring to bend or even break the rules. They might be able to create procedures for other people to follow but will resist following these procedures. They believe there's always a better way to do something. They prefer more creative or varied work.

- "Procedures" colleagues like following the tried and tested approach, and believe that there is a "right" way to do things. They will tend to be happy doing repetitive tasks and generally do not like being interrupted. Colleagues can also be "mainly options," "equally options and procedures," or "mainly procedures."

Question to ask: "Why did you choose your current job/role/career/self-employment?"

Interpreting the response: "Options" colleagues will mention values or criteria (such as "I enjoy it" or "challenge"), or generally indicate that there were possibilities, opportunities, and choice. "Procedures" colleagues will tell you *how* it happened and give you the story (even though the question asks "why"), or they will indicate that there was no choice. A mixture will indicate where the colleague is along the spectrum.

Examples of influencing language:

- Options: Break/bend the rules just for you; opportunity; choice; expanding; options; the sky's the limit; alternatives; possibilities.

- Procedures: The right/proven way; tried and trusted; obligations; also speaking in procedural terms, for example, first, second, then, lastly.

Tips:

- When selling to an "options" buyer, be prepared to give them options and even to make special deals for them. When selling to a "procedures" buyer, tell them the "best" or "right" one for them.

- Consider consumer preferences; call centers where you need to press buttons several times before speaking to a customer-services agent or organizations where the buying process is overly rigid or where no mixing and matching are allowed might deter customers at the "options" end of the spectrum. Equally, unstructured selling methods or presenting too many options might deter customers at the "procedures" end of the spectrum.

- The right way to influence a general audience or an audience you do not know is to use a combination of "options" and "procedures" patterns.

- There are many opportunities for using these patterns and you can probably think of alternative ways yourself. (Notice how this tip is "options" and the previous tip is "procedures.")

4. Frame of reference filter

Overview: How do you find motivation? From external sources, advice and other people, or from your own internal standards and beliefs?

The spectrum: "Internal" (sometimes known as "internally refer-enced") or "external" (sometimes known as "externally referenced").

- "Internal" colleagues set their own standards, provide their own motivation, decide for themselves on the quality of their work, and will take advice only from people who *they* have decided are worth listening to.

- "External" colleagues need other people's opinions and direction in order to be motivated and to know how they are doing.

- Colleagues can also be "mainly internal" (sometimes known as "internal with an external check," that is, they will check with other people just to confirm their own conclusions or ideas), "equally internal and external," or "mainly external" (sometimes known as "external with an internal check," that is, they will check their own thoughts/feelings before accepting other people's opinions and conclusions).

Question to ask: "How do you know you've done a good job [at work]?"

Interpreting the response: "Internal" colleagues will "just know," or indicate (verbally and non-verbally) that they have decided. "External" colleagues will talk about other people (such as their boss or customers) telling them, or about the results showing them. A mixture will indicate where the colleague is along the spectrum.

Examples of influencing language:

- "Internal": Only you can decide; you know it's your choice; what do you think?; you may want to consider; a suggestion for you to think about; it's up to you.

- "External": Others will say; the feedback will be; the recognition you'll get; others will notice; the [information source] reported that...

Tips:

- When managing colleagues, generally the more external they are, the more feedback they will require.

- When planning a project or a piece of work, where possible involve "internal" colleagues at the early stages, so that they can shape or have an input into the plans.

- When presenting to an audience, recognize that there will almost certainly be some "internal" colleagues who will want to decide for themselves whether you are worth listening to. Therefore, for a new audience, mention your credentials when you introduce yourself and use phrases such as "decide for yourself (or "only you will know") which elements will be useful to you."

5. Action filter

Overview: Do you take the initiative or wait for others to initiate before you take action?

The spectrum: "Proactive" and "reactive."

- "Proactive" colleagues tend to act with little or no hesitation or reflection, jump to conclusions without analyzing, and might appear to "bulldoze" their way through people.

- "Reactive" colleagues tend to pause to understand the situation, analyze and reflect, and wait for others to initiate action. At an extreme, they are "inactive" and can suffer from "analysis-paralysis."

- Colleagues can also be "mainly proactive," "equally proactive and reactive," or "mainly reactive."

Question to ask: "When you come to a situation, do you usually act quickly after sizing it up, or do you make a complete study of all the consequences and then act?" Often it is not necessary to ask the question; just listen to the responses to other questions.

Interpreting the response:

- "Proactive" colleagues will answer "act quickly." Generally, they speak in short sentences, speak as if they are in control of their world, and are direct. Their body language can show signs of impatience and inability to sit still for long periods.

- "Reactive" colleagues will reply "do a study first." Often they speak as if the world controls them, with long and convoluted sentences and "passive" rather than "active" language. They often also use conditional language such as "could," "would," and "might." They are generally able to keep still for long periods.

Examples of influencing language:

- "Proactive": Do it; jump in; now; get it done; don't wait; go for it.

- "Reactive": Analyze; think; reflect; understand; assess; consider; wait; could; might.

Tips:

- Though all meta programs can be useful in the right context and therefore there is no inherently problematic meta-program profile, if you are managing someone who is very "proactive," make sure that you keep sufficiently abreast of what they are doing to ensure that they do the things that are appropriate and not go full steam ahead doing something inappropriate (especially if they also have a strong "internal" pattern).

- Once you've done enough thinking about how to use meta programs, just use them ("reactive" then "proactive").

6. Relationship filter

Overview: How do you react to change and how much change do you need? Does your motivation to change come from perceived "sameness" or "difference"?

The spectrum: "Sameness" and "difference."

- "Sameness" colleagues like things to stay the same and do not like change. In a work context, they might accept a major change every 10 years, and generally will seek a change once every 15–25 years. They also notice the similarities to previous or other situations.

- "Difference" colleagues seek radical and frequent change. They get restless every one to two years unless there is change. They will notice the differences from previous or other situations. Some "difference" colleagues can also be "mismatchers," in other words, colleagues who will disagree with what is said or do the opposite of what you ask them to do.

- Colleagues can also be "sameness with exception" (seek major change every 7–15 years), "equally sameness and difference" (every 5–7 years), and "difference with exception" (every 3–5 years).

Question to ask: "What's the relationship between your job/work during this year and during last year?" If they happen to have had a big change within the last year, you could ask instead, "What's the relationship between this job/role and your last job/role?"

Interpreting the response: "Sameness" colleagues will notice how things are *the same* as before. "Sameness with exception" colleagues will notice how things are *similar* to before, or slightly changed. "Difference with exception" colleagues will notice how things have changed. "Difference" colleagues might not even understand the term "relationship" in the question; they will describe how it's completely different, transformed, or revolutionized.

Examples of influencing language:

- "Sameness": Just as before; just like you've always done; identical; unchanged.

- "Sameness with exception": More; better; less; same except; evolving; progress.

- "Sameness" and "difference" equally: a combination of the previous two categories will work.

- "Difference with exception": new; unusual; different; lots of changes.

- "Difference": revolutionary; totally new; brand new; switch; shift; unique; unrecognizable; totally different; completely changed; (or even) you probably won't believe this (for the mismatches).

Tips:

- Many public-sector and private-sector organizations have frequent reorganizations to reflect changing economic or political circumstances. For employees toward the "sameness" end of the spectrum, point out all the elements that will still be the same. Ensure that staff at the "difference" end of the spectrum have sufficient change, even if it means something relatively small like moving them to a new team or office.

- According to the research in *Words That Change Minds*, around two thirds of people fall into the "sameness with exception" category. Therefore, when advertising, it is often more effective to say "improved" when updating an existing product rather than "brand new." Similarly, when there are culture-change initiatives, where possible highlight the similarities with the previous situation.

- Just as in previous filters, the final tip gives the two ends of the spectrum; you might have noticed that the relationship filter has a completely different distribution compared to the previous filters ("sameness" and then "difference" statements).

7. Chunk size filter

Overview: What chunk size of information do you handle well? This links to the Hierarchy of Ideas covered in Chapter 7.

The spectrum: "Global" (also known as "general") and "specific" (also known as "detail").

- "Global" colleagues want the big picture and overview. They might present ideas in a random order. They dislike working with details for a long time.

- "Specific" colleagues like working with small amounts of information (otherwise they may feel overwhelmed) and might get so engrossed in the details that they can't see the wood for the trees. They may find it difficult to prioritize because they see so much detail.

- Colleagues can also be "global to specific" (also called "mainly global") or "specific to global" (also called "mainly specific").

Question to ask: "If we were going to do a project together, would you want to know the big picture or the details first? Would you really need to know the [other, that is, details or big picture, depending on the previous answer]?" Often it is not necessary to ask the question; just listen to how much detail is provided in response to the other questions.

Interpreting the response:

- "Global" colleagues will reply "big picture" to the first question and "no" in response to the second. They usually present ideas in a random order, present summaries/overview, talk about concepts, talk in the abstract, and often use short sentences with few details.

- "Specific" colleagues will reply "details" and "no." When speaking, they usually give sequences, use lots of adverbs/adjectives and, if they lose the sequence, they will start over again.

- "Global to specific" colleagues will answer "big picture" and "yes." "Specific to global" colleagues will answer "details" and "yes." They will both use a combination of the two main traits.

Story 15.2

During the same project mentioned in Story 15.1, I interviewed someone who said he preferred the big picture and didn't want the details. However, he took nearly five minutes to answer the first question about an overview of his role, including two minutes of reflection, and the whole modeling-interview process took seven hours compared to an average of four hours. Needless to say, I noted him as "detailed" (and "reactive"—see "Action filter").

Examples of influencing language:

- "Global": the big picture; essentially; the key aspects; in general; conceptually; idea; concept; typically; overall; overview.
- "Specific": exactly; precisely; specifically; plan; schedule; define and structure; give lots of detail in sequence.

Tips:

- Because the distribution according to the research is "global" at 60 percent, "equal global and specific" at 25 percent, and "specific" at 15 percent, give the big picture first and then give any necessary details later when speaking to a general audience or someone you don't know (with pointers about how to obtain more information).
- Generally, the more senior the role, the more likely it is that the employee will be "global." Therefore, when in meetings or doing presentations, present overviews with key points to senior managers to gain their attention and then use sensory acuity to tell when you're giving them enough, or too much, detail subsequently.

8. Attention direction filter

Overview: Do you display, and respond to, non-verbal behaviors? Are you aware of, and is your attention on, other people?

The spectrum: "Self" and "other."

- "Self" colleagues live more in their internal world. They do not show many emotions, they pay attention only to the content of a communication rather than to any non-verbal elements. They know how a communication is going based on their own feelings.

- "Other" colleagues are more animated and respond to other people with non-verbal language as well as verbal. They know how a communication is going by the non-verbal responses.

- Although there are no specific middle points of this spectrum, there are different degrees of "other." Some NLP schools will refer to "self and other." According to the research, only a small percentage of people at work are "self."

Question to ask: There is no question to elicit this meta program; simply observe responses to other questions. Perhaps sneeze or drop your pen—"self" colleagues will not notice, "other" colleagues will respond accordingly.

Interpreting the response: See previous point.

Examples of influencing language: There is no specific influencing language; for "self" colleagues, keep the communication focused on the content, and for "other" colleagues, make sure that you build and maintain rapport and be willing to communicate non-verbally.

Tips: This is an important meta program for recruitment. Though technical roles might not need "other" patterns, most roles will require a degree of it. Fortunately, only a small percentage of people at work are "self."

Story 15.3

An NLP colleague told me of an airline company that was losing market share and in financial difficulties, largely because its cabin crew were not serving customer needs. The company used this one meta program to help change the situation. All potential recruits were asked to prepare a presentation to deliver to the other candidates, while some of the interviewers were observing at the side of the room. However, unbeknown to the attendees, the interviewers were not observing the speakers; they were observing the audience, looking out for those who had an extreme (almost compulsive) "other" pattern, whose attention was directed solely on the speaker. Subject to other interview requirements, *these* were the people who were hired.

9. Stress response filter

Overview: How do you react to normal levels of stress at work?

The spectrum: "Thinking" (sometimes known as "dissociated"), "feeling" (sometimes known as "associated"), and "choice."

- "Thinking" colleagues (15 percent) do not have emotional responses to normal levels of stress at work. They will not panic and might have difficulty empathizing with colleagues or clients.
- "Feeling" colleagues (15 percent) will have an emotional response and stay emotional; they are not naturally suited to "pressurized" jobs.
- "Choice" colleagues (70 percent) initially have an emotional response but then will be able to return to a more balanced state if they want to. As managers, they can empathize and also be detached as the situation requires.

Question to ask: "Tell me about a situation at work that caused you trouble (or was difficult, or a challenge or problem)."

Interpreting the response:

- "Feeling" colleagues will show signs of emotion and stay in that state. Using sensory acuity (Chapter 5), you would notice changes in breathing, skin tones and color, and body posture and voice tonality, and their eyes will look down (and probably to their left to access kinesthetic—see Chapter 6, eye patterns).
- "Thinking" colleagues will not show signs of emotion.
- "Choice" colleagues will initially show signs of emotion and then vary between showing emotions and not showing emotions (their eyes may look upward some of the time).

Examples of influencing language:

- "Thinking": Clear thinking; logical; rational; hard facts; statistics; figures; evidence.
- "Feeling": Get them feeling a positive emotion (such as excitement, anticipation) about something and then use words like "intense," "exciting," "amazing," "wonderful," and "fantastic."
- "Choice": Use language that covers being excited and being rational, for example, "makes good sense and feels right."

Tips:

- As alluded to earlier, "feeling" clients might not be suited to management because they get stressed, and "thinking" managers might not be able to empathize with staff. "Choice" is a more suitable manager profile.

- Consider the amount of stress involved in a role when selecting a candidate.

10. Affiliation filter

Overview: what kind of environment do you work best in? Alone, having your own responsibilities with others around you, or sharing responsibility?

The spectrum: "Independent," "management," or "team."

- "Independent" colleagues prefer to work alone.

- "Management" colleagues (the majority) prefer to work with other people and have their own area of responsibility.

- "Team" colleagues prefer to work with other people and to have shared responsibility for work.

- Although colleagues will tend to have one preference, it is possible that they might be a mixture of two types, or even three types.

Question to ask: "Tell me about a situation at work that made you happy [or a similar value they have mentioned previously]. What did you like about it?"

Interpreting the response:

- "Independent" colleagues will refer only to themselves, making no mention of other people.

- "Management" colleagues will mention situations when they did the task and that other people were present or involved (it is possible that they might not actually mention anyone else although it is implied by the nature of the situation that other people were involved, for example, doing a presentation or chairing a meeting).

- "Team" colleagues will mention other people and that responsibility was shared, or that "we did it (as a team together)."

Examples of influencing language:

- "Independent": Do it alone; by yourself; total responsibility and control; without interruption.

- "Management": You'll be in charge/direct/lead with others around; you'll be responsible for this, and they'll be responsible for that.

- "Team": We all; us; let's; together; team/joint/group effort; share responsibility; we're all in this together.

Tip: Bear in mind staff's preferences when deciding on office layout and work allocation.

11. Work preference filter

Overview: Do you focus more on thoughts and feelings, or on ideas, systems, and tools when organizing your work?

The spectrum: "Person," "thing," and "system."

- "Person" colleagues prefer to work with people.

- "Thing" colleagues prefer to work with ideas, tools, machines, and tasks. "System" colleagues prefer to work with systems, or when working with people and things, they are interested in how the system works.

- Most people are "thing," "system," or a combination of "person and thing/system."

Question to ask: "Tell me about a situation at work that made you happy [or a similar value they have mentioned previously]. What did you like about it?" Because this is the same question as in the previous meta program, you can ask it for a different situation until you become practiced at listening for both meta programs at the same time.

Interpreting the response:

- "Person" colleagues will mention names, people and, generally, people will be the most important aspect.

- "Thing" colleagues will mention items such as tasks, goals, outcomes; they might imply that people are "objects" in the process.

- "System" colleagues will mention interrelationships between different parts of the process and people.

Examples of influencing language:

- "Person": Use people's names and how they feel; mention the people involved in the situation.
- "Thing": Mention machines, tools, tasks, processes, etc.
- "System": Mention how the wider system works or how the people and things fit together.

Tips:

- Just because someone is "person" it does not mean that they are necessarily nice. It is conceivable that they could be excellent at building rapport and empathizing with people, yet use this skill to manipulate them.
- "Thing" or "system" colleagues will be suited to doing reorganizations where drastic action is needed, because they will not concern themselves with any (temporary) upset that people feel about changes.

12. Management direction filter

Overview: Do you have rules of behavior for yourself and others at work? (This meta program is essential in deciding whether someone will make a good manager.)

The spectrum:

- "Self and others": Have management rules for themselves and for other people, and are willing to tell other people what to do. This is an essential pattern for effective leaders, managers, and advisors, and the research shows that 75 percent of people have this pattern at work.
- "Self only": Can manage their own work but are uninterested in managing others. These people are generally not management material. Only 3 percent of people have this pattern.
- "Others only": Though they are very good at directing and/or managing others, they are not able to manage or direct themselves. This is a typical pattern for bureaucrats or civil servants; 7 percent of people have this pattern.
- "Self but not others": They are able to manage themselves. Though they are able to manage or direct others, they do not

want to ("who am I to tell you/someone else what to do?"). This pattern may be suitable for business and life coaches and counselors, because they are supposed to draw information from their clients rather than give specific advice; 15 percent of people have this pattern.

Questions to ask: There are three questions:

1. "Do you know what you need to do to increase your chances of success at work?"

2. "Do you know what someone else needs to do to increase their chances of success at work?"

3. "Would you find it easy to tell them?"

Interpreting the responses:

- "Self and others": 1) yes, 2) yes, 3) yes.

- "Self only": 1) yes, 2) no (or not interested). The third question is then not relevant.

- "Others only": 1) no (or has difficulty in answering), 2) yes, 3) yes or no.

- "Self but not others": 1) yes, 2) yes, 3) no (or reluctant).

Examples of influencing language:

- Self and others: "If you were me/him/her, you would probably...."

- Self only: "It doesn't matter so much about others as long as you know/are clear."

- Others only: "Though you may not know for yourself what's best, you can inform others of what's best for them."

- Self but not others: "You know what's right for you. Let others decide for themselves."

Tip: The types of role suited to each pattern were mentioned above when explaining this filter (i.e. "self and others": leaders, managers, and advisors; "others only": bureaucrats and civil servants; "self but not others": business/life coaches and counsellors).

13. Convincer representation filter

Overview: What type of information do you need to begin to get convinced of something? (This is the first of two filters relating to how colleagues become convinced.)

The spectrum: as the name suggests, it's either "see," "hear," "experience it/do it," or "read about it."

Question to ask: "How do you know that someone else (e.g. a colleague) is good at what they do? Do you have to see them do it, hear about it, do it with them/experience it, or read about it?"

Interpreting the response: Whichever representational system they give as the answer is the preference.

Examples of influencing language: We will cover this in the following meta program because these two filters are closely linked.

14. Convincer demonstration filter

Overview: At what point in the process do you become convinced?

The spectrum: "Automatic" (automatically convinced, assumes that colleagues are good and gives them the benefit of the doubt), "number of times," "period of time," and "consistent" (never truly convinced).

Question to ask: "How often do you need to see/hear/experience/read about it [depending on the reply to the previous question] before you're *convinced* that someone is good at what they do?"

Interpreting the response: This has been covered in "The spectrum" above. According to the research, slightly more than half of colleagues have a visual/see convincer, around one third have an auditory/hear convincer. Half have a "number of times convincer" (three times is the most common), and a quarter have a "period of time" convincer.

Examples of influencing language:

- "Automatic": You can assume; the benefit of the doubt; decide soon.

- "Number of times": Match their responses. For example, if someone needs to hear about it (convincer representation filter) three times, then either speak to them three times or offer them the contact details of three people (at least) to speak to. It might also be appropriate to use relevant predicates (Chapter 6).

- "Period of time": It has been [period of time stated] since...; it feels like it has been [period of time] since... (even if it hasn't been quite as long as that).

- "Consistent": Since you'll never be truly convinced, the only way to find out is to....

Tips:

- Use the two convincer filters when selling. Many people obtain three quotes when buying something (a three-times convincer pattern is common), or try three items, or possibly take a period of time before deciding to buy something.

- If you are selling to someone with an "automatic" or "one time" convincer, do your best to clinch the deal immediately because they might easily be convinced by the next salesperson! This can apply to ideas within an organization as well as buying products/services.

15. Primary interest filter

Overview: This relates to your main interest in a given event or situation.

The spectrum: "People," "place," "thing," "activity," "time," or "information." This indicates in what a colleague will be most interested in work situations and can be important for job assignment and recruitment.

Question to ask: "Tell me about your favorite restaurant. What do you like about it?"

Interpreting the response (the question in brackets relates to the influencing language):

- "People" (i.e. who?): Mentions who they are with or the staff.

- "Place" (i.e. where?): Describes the geography or location.

- "Thing" (i.e. how or whether?): Mentions the type of food or any theme particularly relevant to the restaurant.

- "Activity" (i.e. what?): Mentions what was happening (e.g. busy waiters, musicians).

- "Time" (i.e. when?): Mentions when they go there.

- "Information" (i.e. why?): Might ask you why you want to know, or give you lots of information about the restaurant.

Influencing language: Meet the preference by answering the question(s) shown in brackets previously. Using a project as an example, for "information," give the colleague reasons why the project will go ahead and relevant information, such as the history, cost, and systems to be used in the project. For "people," tell the colleague who will be involved in the project.

Summary

Tip 15.2

Assuming that you have not been formally trained in how to use meta programs, I suggest that you initially focus your efforts in understanding your own meta-program profile. If you want to use this book to understand others, I suggest that you break the task down into bite-size chunks, either:

- Pick one person and understand (or, if they are willing, elicit) their meta programs.
- Pick one specific meta program and notice how the behaviors of people at work reflect that filter.

Please also be aware that everything is relative; for example, if you happen to be very "options" orientated, then someone who is "equally options and procedures" might appear to be very "procedures" to you.

Tip 15.3

Often you will be able to estimate someone's specific meta-program pattern just by listening to their language. For example, if someone frequently talks about their problems and what they don't want, you could reasonably guess that they are near the "away from" end of the "Direction filter" spectrum.

Following on from Tip 15.2, Exercise 15.1 will help you deepen your understanding of meta programs.

Exercise 15.1

Elicit your own meta-program profile using the following table.

1. Values

"What do you want in/what's important to you about your work?"

2. Direction Filter

"Why are these criteria/values important to you?"
Ask 3 times.

__ Toward	__ Mainly away
__ Mainly toward	__ Away from
__ Equal	

3. Reason Filter

"Why did you choose your current work/job?"

__ Options	__ Mainly procedures
__ Mainly options	__ Procedures
__ Equal	

4. Frame of Reference

"How do you know you've done a good job?"

__ Internal	__ Mainly external
__ Mainly internal	__ External
__ Equal	

5. Action

"When you come to a situation, do you usually act quickly after sizing it up, or do you make a complete study of all the consequences and then act?"

Or just listen to responses to other questions.

__ Proactive   __ Mainly reactive

__ Mainly proactive   __ Reactive

__ Equal

6. Relationship

"What's the relationship between your job (or work) this year and last year?"

__ Sameness   __ Difference with exception

__ Sameness with exception   __ Equal

__ Difference

7. Chunk Size

"If we were going to do a project together, would you want to know the big picture or the details first? Would you really need to know the [other]?"

Or just listen to responses to other questions.

__ Global   __ Specific to global

__ Global to specific   __ Specific

8. Attention Direction

No question, just observe (e.g. drop pen, sneeze).

__ Self   __ Other

__ Equal

9. Emotional Stress Response

"Tell me about a situation at work that gave you trouble, a one-time event."

__ Thinking   __ Feeling

__ Choice

10. Affiliation

"Tell me about a situation at work that was happy [or a value mentioned]. What did you like about it?"

__ Independent   __ Team

__ Management

11. Work Preference

(Could answer from the previous question) "Tell me about a situation (in relevant context) that was happy [or a value mentioned]. What did you like about it?"

__ Person __ System

__ Thing

12. Management Direction

"Do you know what you need to do to increase your chances of success at work?"

"Do you know what someone else needs to do to increase their chances of success at work?"

"Would you find it easy to tell them?"

__ Self and others (yes; yes; yes)

__ Self only (yes; no/disinterested; not relevant)

13. Convincer Representation

"How do you know that someone else (a colleague) is good at what they do?" ("Do you need to see, hear, do/experience, or read about?")

__ See __ Do/experience

__ Hear __ Read

14. Convincer Demonstration

"How often do you need to [answer 13] to be *convinced* they're good?"

__ Automatic __ Duration

__ Number __ Consistent

15. Primary Interest

"Tell me about your favorite restaurant. What do you like about it?"

__ Place __ Activity

__ People __ Information

__ Thing __ Time

__ Others only (no; yes; yes/no)

__ Self but not others (yes; yes; no/reluctant)

Applications for individual use

Many of the tips provided earlier can be used when dealing with individuals. More specifically, meta programs can be used in the following contexts:

- **Selling:** Understanding or recognizing even a few meta programs will give you an insight into how best to approach a customer.

- **Coaching and management:** Choosing the best approach to motivate and communicate with clients and staff. Also, where appropriate, you could inform your colleagues or coaching/consultancy clients about some or all of the meta programs, so that they can better understand their work contacts. Story 15.4 provides a useful example.

- **Interviews:** Being able to understand and influence candidates or interviewers.

- **Conflicts and misunderstandings:** It is common for disagreements to be caused by people having differences in specific meta-program profiles. You can use the information in this chapter to at least understand the other person and, ideally, to agree on a way to work effectively given any inherent differences.

Story 15.4

I was coaching a very bright managing director, who had challenges regarding some members of her staff. I elicited her meta programs (using a sheet similar to that shown in Exercise 15.1) and then explained to her each of the filters and where she was on each spectrum/category. She was enthralled and said, "I wish I'd known this 20 years ago. I would have been a far better manager."

Applications within organizations

There are numerous applications in groups and organizations, as well as those already mentioned in the tips for each pattern:

- **Advertising and marketing:** Use "improved" ("sameness with exception") rather than "brand new" ("difference") when launching upgrades or updates to existing products because most people are "sameness with exception."

- **Presentations:** As alluded to in several of the filters, use a combination of influencing language for certain patterns to help ensure that you reach the whole audience.

- **Recruitment:** Profile the job/role using meta programs to decide on your ideal profile and acceptable alternatives for the role, and then use appropriate influencing language in the job adverts. Also, elicit the key meta programs during interviews.

- **Team building:** As with "values" in Chapter 14, help members of the team to understand the meta-program patterns generally, and in particular where their colleagues fit along the spectra.

Part V

Replicating Excellence With NLP

Chapter 16 explains some of the key aspects of the NLP modeling methodology and how to use the techniques covered in this book when modeling excellence. It also briefly describes how to identify and use a particular aspect of people's thought processes, known as "strategies."

Modeling

How to replicate excellence at work

Don't reinvent the wheel, just realign it.
—Anthony J. D'Angelo, author, educational entrepreneur

"Why reinvent the wheel?" is a phrase often used in businesses. If the processes or tasks you require are done really well by colleagues or elsewhere, you can use a methodology developed in the NLP field to replicate the excellence. This is known as "modeling," which is one of the three key benefits of NLP (see Chapter 1). Similarly, if you can do a particular activity excellently in one context and would like to do so in another, you can use the NLP modeling process to help you replicate your own excellence.

This chapter presents only some key elements of modeling within the context of the other chapters in this book.

Why is modeling so useful at work?

Modeling can help organizations to keep their performance in line with, or ahead of, that of their competitors and it can help to improve individual and team performances in areas such as:

- Problem solving.
- Creativity.
- Business process design.
- Presentations.
- Selling.
- Recruitment.

Modeling can help you to learn far more quickly than if you attempted to learn without the modeling framework. At an organizational level, this reduces the time required for training.

Key concepts and background

One of the NLP Presuppositions is that if someone in a broadly similar situation to yours can do something, then you can learn to do it ("Modeling excellence leads to improved performance," page 42). This chapter talks about how to do this.

Pareto's law (named after the Italian economist, Vilfredo Pareto) states that 80 percent of results come from 20 percent of effort, or in the workplace, 20 percent of the people. The co-developers of NLP, Bandler and Grinder, wanted to find out what was the difference that made the difference between excellent performance and merely good performance. Initially, they studied and modeled excellent communication skills found in leading therapists. Since then, they and many other NLP professionals have modeled a wide variety of business and non-business skills.

Though it might be possible to "mimic" the physical activities that are done by excellent presenters, engineers, or managers simply by observing them, a key belief in NLP is that what happens inside the minds of excellent performers is the difference that makes the difference.

An overview of the modeling process

At its simplest, modeling can be broken down into the following key steps:

1. Find someone (an expert) who is excellent at something you want to excel at or replicate.

2. Find out the expert's internal processes such as their beliefs, meta programs in the context, and values. You could use the Neurological Levels model to find out their thoughts and feelings about the task they excel at. Eliciting their submodalities could also be useful (the sections headed "Finding experts" and "Gaining the information" discuss this in more detail, including what to do if you do not have access to the expert).

3. Where possible, observe them doing the task, that is, the actual behaviors, because people who are excellent at something are

not always fully aware of exactly what they are doing at certain points in the process.

4. Find out their internal states, that is, how they are feeling, when they do the task.

5. Adopt their ways and strategies of thinking and feeling (steps 2, 3, and 4 above), refining them until you are able to replicate, or even improve on, their results (strategies are considered in more detail at the end of this chapter). Depending on the amount of time and resources available for the modeling project, you would want to make at least significant improvements in your results.

6. Train other people to adopt this model and hence improve their results.

Some considerations when modeling

Here are some areas to consider before and during a modeling project. This section is written as though you are the decision maker in this regard for your organization:

- **Your desired outcome:** The first Principle for Success (page 44) emphasizes the importance of knowing what you want from the modeling project. This will influence, or may be constrained by, the amount of time and resources (money, skills, and people) available to do the project.

Tip 16.1

It is important to be specific about what you want to model and, if necessary, chunk the process down into details. For example, modeling an excellent salesperson could be useful; it would probably be more useful to model specific aspects of the sales process from different experts such as sales research, canvassing, appointment making, initial meetings,

handling objections, closing the sale, and relationship management after the sale.

- **Available resources:** Following on from the previous point,
  a full-scale modeling project can be time-consuming and
  labor-intensive. How do the costs compare to the likely
  benefits? Do you (or the team) have the necessary modeling skills or would you need assistance from consultants
  experienced in NLP-based modeling? As a reader of this
  book, even if you have not been formally NLP trained, you
  will be able to gain a certain amount of information about
  experts' values, beliefs, and meta programs, as well as ask
  relevant questions, use the Neurological Levels model, and
  have an understanding of state and its importance in doing
  a task well.

- **Finding experts:** Finding people who are truly excellent and
  who are willing and able to devote the time to be modeled can
  sometimes be challenging. If you are modeling in-house experts (for example, salespeople), though you might be able to
  "insist" or persuade the experts to take part, there is no guarantee that they will willingly do so. They might wish to keep
  their "secrets."

  If you are modeling people who you do not have access to,
  you will need to make the most of available information, while
  recognizing that the project might not yield the same level of
  results as other forms of modeling projects (see the following
  section, "Gaining the information").

  You would also ideally have several experts, so that you
  could identify what is essential and what is idiosyncratic. You
  might also want to have a group of models who are good, but
  not excellent, against whom to compare what the expert does.
  Please be sensitive about how you explain the project to the
  comparison group.

- **Gaining the information:** There are several possible methods,
  such as interviews (structured, semi-structured, informal),

direct observation and indirect observation (videos). Although it is clearly more effective to be able to model someone who you have access to and who is willing to be modeled, in his series of books called *Strategies of Genius* Robert Dilts did extensive modeling projects on people who are deceased, such as Wolfgang Amadeus Mozart, Walt Disney, and Aristotle. Though, clearly, Dilts was unable to gain information in the ways mentioned in this section, he was able to analyze quotations and anecdotes to gain insights into the thinking processes of these geniuses, and then demonstrate how these could be used to develop and improve creativity and ability to solve problems.

- **Using the information:** Ideally, you would consider how you would use the information for you personally or for your organization before starting the project. Possible uses include improving recruitment, and staff training and performance.

Story 16.1

The situation mentioned in Story 15.1 happened during a modeling project. Essentially, I and my colleagues looked at what was the difference between effective salespeople and those who were not so successful for a particular organization. The purpose was to create an easy-to-use model of what made a successful salesperson in that company, so that the company could recruit accordingly. We each interviewed a selected group, asking them questions about each of the different Neurological Levels, as well as eliciting values and criteria equivalents, meta programs, and key beliefs, and also using the perceptual-positions approach to see how they saw other stakeholders. Certain clear patterns emerged, which helped the company to recruit and promote more effectively.

Once you have decided the purpose of the modeling project, follow the six steps mentioned in the section, "An overview of the modeling process," on page 232.

Strategies

Step 5 of the modeling process mentions strategies. "Strategy" in NLP has a slightly different meaning from that in everyday use. "Strategies" can be a complex NLP topic, which is best understood by means of a live training course; the following is a very brief summary so, if you want to find out more, refer to the "Resources for further learning" section.

From an NLP perspective, a strategy is a sequence of information gathered externally (using the main representational systems) and processed internally (also using the main representational systems) that leads to a specific result. People have strategies for almost everything they do, for example, making buying decisions, deciding when it's time to close a sale, and becoming motivated to take action.

Why are strategies useful?

Some of the benefits of knowing about strategies are:

- You can learn how to model your own excellence; for example, how do you make excellent decisions?
- You can learn how to understand other people's decision-making processes; this can help you to influence them.

In addition, NLP strategies can be used to help people change their own strategies if they are not helpful, for example, if someone finds making decisions difficult, or to create a strategy if someone doesn't have an existing one. However, it is important to note that these topics are outside the scope of this book and require NLP Practitioner-level training.

Identifying strategies

For the purposes of explaining strategies in the context of modeling at work, let's use the example of making purchasing decisions in order to describe the principles. Most people have a process they repeatedly go through to make decisions to buy something, known in NLP as their "decision-making strategy." So when you make a decision about, for example, which briefcase to buy, you will go through a sequence that will include some or all of the following, in no particular order (you might wish to refer to representational systems in Chapter 6):

- Looking at the briefcase (visual external).
- Discussing it with the salesperson (auditory external).
- Touching/using/trying it (kinesthetic external).
- Checking that it meets your requirements, for example, size, color, number of compartments, price, brand, etc. (auditory digital).
- Visualizing how it would look when you use it (visual internal constructed).
- Remembering what your old briefcase looked like (visual internal remembered).
- Imagining what people would say about it if you bought it (auditory internal constructed).
- Remembering what people have said about your old briefcase (auditory internal remembered).
- How you would feel about buying it (kinesthetic internal).

As an example, someone's decision-making strategy could be:

1. See it (visual external).
2. Check that it has all the features and is the right price (auditory digital).
3. Pick it up, hold it, and carry it (kinesthetic external).
4. Imagine what you would look like carrying it into a business meeting (visual internal constructed).
5. Repeat the process with some other briefcases.
6. Check again the price and the guarantee (auditory digital).
7. Feel good about buying it (kinesthetic internal).
8. Buy it.

Exercise 16.1

Remember times when you made decisions that you were happy with, and identify the sequence you usually go through (based on the previous bullet points) to make these good decisions. This will provide you with a template that you can use for making decisions in the future (i.e. your decision-making strategy). Please ensure that you choose times when you were *happy* with the decision you made and, ideally, when you were alone (you want to identify *your* strategy, not someone else's).

It is worth being aware that making decisions can often be broken down into the following components.

1. Being motivated to actually make a decision (to buy a briefcase). This will take a period of time; from an NLP perspective, it is considered to be a separate strategy that takes place before you actually go into the shop (or Website) to buy. This stage usually includes choosing the specification or criteria for the product or service you are buying.

2. Selecting/deciding on which briefcase you will buy (when you are in the shop or online).

3. Becoming convinced that this briefcase is right for you before choosing. You might find that you repeat the process detailed in the previous point several times or over a period of time before deciding, for example, testing four briefcases. This is step 5 in the briefcase example earlier. This often links to a person's "convincer demonstration" meta program (page 220-221).

Sometimes a fourth component relates to how someone becomes reassured that it was a good decision/purchase. Ideally, this would take place before the decision has been finally made; for example, some people might discuss the purchase with a friend before the end of the refund period. Using the briefcase example, step 6 (and possibly step 7) could be the reassurance element.

Where decisions are made by groups within organizations, similar principles will usually apply. Decision-making processes and strategies might vary depending on the importance of the decision (or the cost of the product).

Applications of decision strategies at work

Even with this brief introduction to strategies, there are several ways that you can use this information in business:

- **Making decisions.** Identify your own decision-making strategy, so that you can replicate it and use it as a checklist.

Story 16.2

I taught this material to a coaching client who, as an entrepreneur, wanted to make consistently good decisions and stop making occasional bad decisions. He identified his effective decision-making strategy and also the process he followed when he made poor decisions and, having recognized the difference, he was able to ensure that he followed the effective model every time.

- **Selling.** If appropriate and possible, casually ask prospects about things they have bought (such as car, watch, clothes, rings) and how they decided that the item was for them. This will give you an indication of their decision-making strategy. As much as possible, present your offering in the representational-system sequence that matches their strategy. This might not necessarily lead to the prospect's agreeing to buy your product if it is not right for them; it will, however, increase the likelihood of their making a faster decision. Most sales professionals prefer a quick decision from prospects, so that even if it's a "no" they can quickly move on to the next prospect.

- **Influencing colleagues.** If you want a colleague to make a decision, as with the previous point, present information about your offering in the representational-system sequence that matches their strategy.

Part VI

Applying NLP at Work

Chapter 17 looks at 16 areas of work, covered in Chapter 1, and summarizes the main NLP techniques to use in each area. It is intended as a quick reminder to help you plan and prepare for these types of work activity.

Applications of NLP

Reference guide when using NLP for specific work activities

In most of the chapters in the first four parts of this book, you learned about a specific NLP topic in each chapter and how to apply it in various situations in business and the workplace. Chapter 16 covered how to use some of the NLP techniques to model excellence. In this chapter, we will approach this from the opposite direction, that is, we will take each of the 16 work areas and activities referred to in Chapter 1 and briefly look at which of the NLP tools and techniques would be useful for each, together with any other relevant guidelines. The chapter is intended mainly as a reference guide when planning or preparing for any of these activities.

The work activities have been divided into three categories: internal communications, external communications, and work processes, in order to assist you.

Internal communications (with staff and colleagues):

1. Management of staff.
2. Team building.
3. Leadership.
4. Human resources, recruitment, and interviewing.
5. Training.
6. Coaching.

External communications (with customers, clients, and suppliers):

7. Sales, business development, and account management.
8. Marketing and advertising.

9. Liaison with clients, customers, patients, and other service users.

10. Procurement.

11. Negotiation.

12. Presentations.

13. Resolving conflicts and misunderstandings.

Work processes:

14. Consultancy, including change management.

15. Improved decision-making.

16. Creative problem solving.

The foundations

The information in Chapters 2 to 7 represents the communication, goal setting, and mindset fundamentals that will be useful in *all* work situations. They are:

- NLP Presuppositions.
- The Principles for Success.
- Being "At Cause" (these first three points make up the "mindset for success").
- The NLP Communication Model.
- Setting "well-formed," SMARTER goals.
- Sensory acuity.
- Rapport.
- Representational systems.
- Predicates.
- Eye patterns.
- Language: the Hierarchy of Ideas, linguistic presuppositions, small words with big meanings, abstract language (the Milton Model), specific language and power questions (the Meta Model), and metaphors, stories, and analogies.

You have covered these so you now understand their application in all the situations described so far, so when discussing the 16 activities, I will mention these again only when they are particularly helpful or relevant.

In addition, being in a resourceful state (anchoring, Chapter 10) and/ or altering your submodalities to have a positive internal representation of an event or situation (Chapter 9) might be useful to you. Again, because you now understand these techniques, they will not be mentioned unless particularly relevant.

Overview of the 16 activities

For each activity, the NLP techniques and interventions that are particularly applicable (and the relevant chapter) will be mentioned. This will be done in bullet-point format wherever possible to make it easy for you to refer to, because you already have read and therefore understood the relevant information (you might, of course, wish to quickly refresh your memory by revisiting the relevant chapter). There is some duplication because elements of some work activities are similar to those of others (for example, procurement and negotiation); the duplication will also enable you in the future to look at any of the 16 topics without referring to others.

1. Management of staff

Values (Chapter 14): At the annual appraisal for each staff member, set the scene before doing the values-elicitation process (steps 1–5) and eliciting the criteria equivalents for all of the values. After the appraisal, keep your word by doing whatever you can as manager to help each member of your staff to have their values fulfilled, subject to the constraints that you would already have explained to your staff, for example, budgetary limits.

Goal setting (Chapter 4): Set "well-formed" (or SMARTER) goals at annual appraisal time and possibly at project-initiation meetings.

Meta programs (Chapter 15): Identify some of the key meta programs for each employee, so that you have a greater understanding of how they think and respond under different scenarios, and of how to influence them accordingly.

Perceptual positions (Chapter 11): Where relevant, before meeting individual members of staff, do the perceptual-positions exercise to gain an appreciation of their point of view. If a staff member wants or needs to gain insight into another perspective, for example, if there is a conflict with a colleague, take the staff member through the perceptual-positions exercise.

Reframing (Chapter 12) and Changing beliefs conversationally (Chapter 13): Being able to change a member of staff's mindset about a particular situation will be useful at times, for example, feeling negative toward a particular work challenge or colleague.

2. Team building

Goal setting (Chapter 4): Agree on a "well-formed" (SMARTER) goal that the whole team can work toward.

Values (Chapter 14): If the team is ready for it (i.e. if the team is already functioning well), ask the team to list their own values and the criteria equivalents, and share with other team members so that every member has a greater understanding of how to motivate (and avoid demotivating) each other. If team members have been suitably trained, they could do the elicitation process on each other and give feedback to the group. Also, if the team were ready for it, you could elicit team values and the criteria equivalents in the group, so that the team would have a set of values that it collectively created, which would probably enhance team effectiveness and cohesion.

Meta programs (Chapter 15): Explain to the group about some key relevant meta programs, so that they have an understanding that their colleagues might be different and of how to communicate to get the best from each other. For example, two team members' knowledge that one of them is "toward" and the other is "away from" (Direction filter, page 203) might help them understand each other's responses and see the respective benefits, rather than possibly feeling frustrated.

Neurological Levels (Chapter 8): Consider the team's purpose/mission, create a team identity, agree on the team's values, and identify suitable capabilities and behaviors and how they would like the environment to be.

3. Leadership

Neurological Levels (Chapter 8): The leadership exercise (Exercise 8.2, page 130) is a really useful way to gain a greater perspective on your own leadership role. Also, with the abstract language in Chapter 7, being able to clearly know and articulate the organization's mission is essential for a business leader.

Perceptual positions (Chapter 11): According to stories I have heard on training courses, before making important leadership related decisions, Andrew Carnegie would sit in the seats of the other board members (when the boardroom was empty!) and see the situation from the perspective of each director before making his decision. Even if this is not physically possible, you can still do the perceptual-positions process in a different location, creating several position 2s (one for each of the main people or groups affected by the decision).

Reframing (Chapter 12): At times, leaders will need to put a positive spin on situations by turning a seemingly negative situation (such as poor financial results or the closing of a subsidiary) into a more positive one.

4. Human resources, recruiting, and interviewing

Neurological Levels (Chapter 8): Be aware of how the HR policy can support and align with the organization's objectives and mission, identity etc. In particular, ensure that the recruitment policy aligns with the Neurological Levels elements and provide training to ensure that the competencies (i.e. capabilities and behaviors) are appropriate to meet the organization's needs.

Values (Chapter 14): Eliciting the values of the candidate and comparing them with the values required by the role (and indeed the organization's values) will help you recruit more effectively. A phrase often used by HR professionals when discussing recruitment is "recruit for attitude (i.e. values and beliefs), train for skills."

Meta programs (Chapter 15): When seeking to fill a vacancy, do a meta-program profile of the position, listing the key meta-program filters that will be useful, your preferred option on the spectrum, and acceptable alternatives for each of the filters. You would then use relevant influencing language in job adverts and elicit the key meta programs of the candidates during the interview.

Anchoring (Chapter 10): Using your resource anchor will help you be in a positive state for the interview, whether as interviewer or interviewee.

Perceptual positions (Chapter 11): As a candidate (or interviewer), going through the perceptual-positions exercise will help you prepare for the kind of questions an interviewer (or candidate) is likely to ask, and for the kind of information you will be expected to know.

5. Training

When running a training course, it is essential to accommodate the different learning styles of the delegates. Though there are different theories of learning styles, one that many NLP Trainers have found to be particularly useful is based on Bernice McCarthy's "Learning Styles Inventory." Essentially, it states that people have a preferred learning style, and that:

- 35 percent need/prefer to know "why" the material is important.
- 22 percent need/prefer to know the information (i.e. the "what").
- 18 percent need/prefer to learn by doing (i.e. the "how").
- 25 percent need/prefer to learn by self-discovery (i.e. exploring "what-if " scenarios).

This is known as the "4-Mat" system, in which people learn based on all of these four concepts. Although this is not a specific NLP technique, it is taught in many business-related NLP courses and is used as a required structure for presentations in many certified NLP Trainers' training courses. In order to run an effective training segment, it is extremely useful to structure it as follows:

- Give an overview and very brief introduction of the topic to be covered.
- **Why:** Explain **from the trainees' perspective** why this information is so useful to **them** (you may need to use perceptual-positions thinking, that is, positions 2 and 3, to do this). This grabs their attention and engages them. For example, if you are training a group of newly promoted managers in appraisal skills, you would probably mention how doing excellent appraisals will boost staff performance and hence reflect well on them as managers, enhancing their own career prospects.
- **What:** Present the information you want to give them, such as relevant history, theories, facts, figures, processes, and demonstrations.

- **How:** Although the process is explained and possibly demonstrated during the "what" segment, the "how" segment gives the delegates the opportunity to try it in practice and is the active-learning segment.

- **What if:** This is where you explore what the delegates learned during the exercise and how they can use this knowledge in real situations at work. I also ask delegates to keep a learning log of the key points they have learned, how they are going to use the material (when and with whom). In doing this, delegates are future-pacing themselves, putting the material into practice so that the training becomes even more useful.

Representational systems (Chapter 6): wherever possible, present information using the four main representational systems, that is:

- **Visual:** Use a combination of videos, flip charts, PowerPoint, and diagrams. I personally prefer using flip charts to PowerPoint (writing neatly and using colors and diagrams if possible), which are then used as wall charts so that people have a visual reminder throughout the course. Slides are only temporary.

- **Auditory:** There is a natural auditory element to training because you will be speaking. Allow and encourage appropriate verbal interactions and discussion. Consider using music during break times or during certain exercises.

- **Kinesthetic:** Where possible, allow delegates to do exercises or tasks that are relevant to the topic. Also, writing their learning log is to some degree a kinesthetic activity.

- **Auditory digital:** Provide facts and figures where appropriate.

Anchoring (Chapter 10), Submodalities (Chapter 9), and Changing beliefs (Chapter 13): Experienced trainers usually know how to manage their own state. Sometimes non-trainers with a particular specialism are asked to run training segments and might feel somewhat nervous and/or have a negative belief about the event. Use your resource anchor, submodalities of positive experiences, and change any limiting beliefs to help you be in the right mindset to deliver the session.

Perceptual positions (Chapter 11): If you are not sure what the audience wants or what questions they might have (because, for example, you do not have the opportunity to speak with delegates before the segment), then put yourself into positions 2 and 3 to gain some insight into this.

6. Coaching

Coaching as a profession has expanded greatly since the beginning of the new millennium. There are numerous courses, books, and professional coaching associations and, increasingly, managers in the workplace are being encouraged to adopt a coaching style of management. One particularly useful coaching model is known as the GROW model (see "Resources for Further Learning"). This stands for:

- **G**oal: What do you want to achieve? What do you want from the coaching relationship and/or session?

- **R**eality: What's the current situation? Where are you now in relation to achieving your goal?

- **O**ptions: What options do you have to move from where you are to where you want to be, to achieve your goal?

- **W**hat, **W**hen: What will you do? When will you do it?

The "foundations" referred to earlier in this chapter (page 244) are relevant when coaching, and in particular:

- **Communication (Chapter 2):** Explain the Communication Model to the person being coached if they have communication challenges in their work.

- **The "mindset for business success" (Chapter 3):** I explain "Cause and Effect" to every client at the start of the first session, because it is far easier to coach someone if they accept this principle. I **strongly recommend** that you do this. Also, you can mention any relevant NLP Presuppositions during the coaching session and inform the person being coached of the Principles for Success as part of your coaching.

- **Goal setting (Chapter 4):** This forms the "G" and the "R" of the GROW model; it would usually be covered in some depth in the initial session so that you know what the person being coached wants to achieve. In subsequent sessions, you would usually only want to know what the person being coached wants from the session rather than going through the whole goal-setting process again.

- **Meta programs (Chapter 15):** You can use meta programs to gain a greater understanding of the person being coached, and to use the relevant influencing language.

The "Options" segment of the GROW model usually forms the bulk of a coaching session. The NLP techniques covered in Part III and Chapter 14 help you to build on the "O" to help the person being coached overcome obstacles and to move onward faster than they otherwise would.

You can use power questions (Chapter 7, page 112) to be specific about what the person being coached will do and when (the "W").

7. Sales, business development, and account management

Rapport (Chapter 5): This is particularly important in selling, as generally people buy only from people they trust and feel comfortable with, which is usually the result of the salesperson having built rapport with the customer.

Questioning skills (Chapter 7): There are several models and methods for selling, most (if not all) of them relying on the ability of the salesperson to elicit information about factors such as:

- The current situation.
- Any problems the organization is experiencing.
- The implications of these problems, including what it is costing the client or prospect to have the problem/not have the solution.
- The procurement processes within the organization, including who (else) is involved in the decision making.

Values (Chapter 14): It is essential to find out what the client or prospect wants from a supplier and what's important to them/what they look for in the product or service. The values-elicitation process and criteria equivalents will help you immensely. Also, if you know exactly what the client/prospect wants or needs, *and* you can demonstrate how you can meet (or even exceed) these needs, then it ceases to become "selling" and becomes more about "serving," which is what great salesmanship is really about.

Meta programs (Chapter 15): Find out some of the client's or prospect's key meta-program filters (particularly filters 1 to 7 (pages 203–213) and the Convincer filters 13 and 14 (pages 220)) in order to be able to adjust your sales pitch to suit the specific client(s) you are dealing with.

Handling objections and reframing (Chapter 12) and possibly Changing beliefs (Chapter 13): It is rare for clients or prospects not to have objections, so being able to handle objections is a key part of selling. If by some chance you have doubts about your abilities as a salesperson, review Chapter 13.

Perceptual positions (Chapter 11): Being able to "second position" a client/prospect before, during, or after meetings will lead to greater awareness of their perspective and aid the sales process. Similarly, being able to take a "third position" will help give you insights into ways to move forward. The "Disney" process for creative solutions (page 166–167) could be useful.

Knowing your purpose and mission (Chapter 8): While doing the sales-modeling project referred to in Story 15.1 (page 205) and in Story 15.2 (page 212), I noticed that the successful salespeople had a very clear sense of **who else** (i.e. mission, purpose) they were serving in the course of their sales role. It wasn't just the individual customer, or their own family; these successful salespeople knew how their product benefited a wider group, such as the clients of their clients, the whole business community, and even society as a whole. This gave them added motivation to succeed and a sense of congruence with what they were doing, which would have been perceived by clients.

Submodalities (Chapter 9) and Anchoring (Chapter 10): Adjusting your submodalities might be useful before business meetings with important clients or prospects, and you can use your resource anchor before or during meetings. When asking for the sale, it is generally useful to keep quiet; nerves can tempt people to speak, so firing your "calm/relaxed" anchor will help. Also, it might be useful to anchor relevant states in prospects or clients, or use spatial anchors to improve your communication.

Decision-making strategies (Chapter 16): When possible, identify the decision-making strategy of your prospect and present information to them in the order and sequence in which they like to receive the information.

8. Marketing and advertising

Representational systems and predicates (Chapter 6): When advertising, if appropriate, you can use the information in Chapter 6 to engage the senses of the target clients/customers, including using predicates from all four main representational systems.

Anchoring (Chapter 10): Seek to create an association between the product/service you are selling and "good" feelings for the client. Such feelings could include feeling successful, sexy, amused, and upbeat.

Values (Chapter 14): When doing market research, asking questions to elicit and rank values could be useful.

Meta programs (Chapter 15): Use the appropriate influencing language for the key meta programs that relate to your product or service, for example, insurance products are inherently "away from" products (i.e. minimizing or reducing liabilities in the event of a problem). Also, the "Relationship filter" (page 210) mentions that most people prefer "sameness with exception" and hence prefer words such as "improved" rather than "brand new" for most goods. Launches of technology goods may be exceptions to this, where businesses might be seeking to attract "early adopters" (i.e. people who will seek the latest gadget), based on Professor Rodgers' model explained in *Diffusions of Innovation*.

9. Liaison with clients, customers, patients, and other service users

Rapport (Chapter 5): This is particularly important in client-liaison or customer-liaison roles, as generally client satisfaction is enhanced when they deal with customer-liaison staff they trust and feel comfortable with, which is usually the result of the staff having built rapport with the customer.

Perceptual positions (Chapter 11): This will help you to prepare for conversations, and see the client's point of view.

Meta programs (Chapter 15) and Values (Chapter 14): Elicit or listen out for key meta programs and values, to be able to influence more effectively.

Handling objections (Chapter 12): Even if they are mild objections or complaints, the processes described in Chapter 12 will help you to reframe them.

Chunking (Chapter 7): Chunking up could help you to understand what the customer really wants. Chunking down could help you be specific or get the specific information required to help the customer. Chunking laterally could help you reach creative solutions to challenges.

Please also see "Sales" (point 7) and "Resolving conflicts" (point 13).

10. Procurement

Procurement is, in many respects, the flip side of the "sales" coin, and will have a negotiation element (point 11). Although it is often assumed that the client has all the power, this may not always be the case. It is also important to remember that procurement departments usually have "internal" clients, that is, the departments on whose behalf they are procuring; the information about the topics that follow can be used in such situations.

One of my Master Practitioner students had a career in procurement. She said that NLP helped her to recognize what the salespeople, who often have significant amounts of NLP-based training (whether or not it is branded as NLP), were doing during the sales and negotiation process, especially their use of language patterns. This enabled her, for example, to counter some of their statements or probe further (using power questions).

The following points assume that you are sourcing from an organization that has a similar degree of "power" to your organization. Though it is possible for powerful organizations to "bully" suppliers, it is probably not a useful tactic for long-term relationship building, or for procuring from equally powerful, or more powerful, suppliers.

Rapport (Chapter 5): This will help you to negotiate more effectively (see point 11) and perhaps gain preferential treatment in the event of, for example, supply problems.

Power questions (Chapter 7): This will enable you to ask detailed questions, for example, to find out whether the supplier really does have the expertise and experience you are looking for or whether they are being "creative" with the truth.

Values (Chapter 14): Finding out what is important to the supplier (apart from simply "selling") can be useful. For example, if they want to gain a foothold in a particular sector, and if your organization is in that sector, you could use it as a bargaining tool for better service or price. Also, you can use the values-elicitation process to know exactly what you want from the product or service you are procuring.

Meta programs (Chapter 15): During conversations, knowing the profile of the sales representative could help you during the procurement process.

Perceptual positions (Chapter 11): Being able to "second position" a supplier before, during, or after meetings will lead to greater awareness of their perspective and aid the procurement process. Similarly, being able to take a "third position" will help give you insights into ways to move forward.

Handling objections and reframing (Chapter 12): Just as clients might have objections, suppliers might have objections to your proposals, so being able to handle objections is a key part of procurement.

11. Negotiation

Negotiations could take place in a traditional selling/procurement process; please review points 7 and 10 for tips. Apart from these situations, negotiations could take place in a variety of other situations, such as trade-union pay negotiations; remuneration when you join a company, get promoted, or are at an appraisal; or deciding which members of staff can take days off at Christmas in a particular year.

Rapport (Chapter 5): In general, having the capability to create a feeling of trust and co-operation, especially at tense moments, will help you to negotiate more effectively.

Hierarchy of Ideas (Chapter 7): Being able to chunk up to agree on a common objective is usually an essential part of negotiations, and to be able to chunk laterally can help to generate creative solutions or overcome impasses. One negotiation model often taught in NLP is to be able to chunk up high enough until both parties agree, and then chunk down only as quickly as you can continue to maintain agreement and rapport.

Power questions (Chapter 7): Asking questions to uncover details, for example, to find out what specifically the counter-party wants, or what exactly is being offered and expected of you, for example, if you are being promoted.

Submodalities (Chapter 9): If you feel uncomfortable about negotiating with someone more senior than you at work, you might want to adjust your submodalities relating to that person to "shrink them down to size."

Anchoring (Chapter 10): As with the previous point, you could use your resource anchor to feel resourceful (powerful, confident, etc.) during the negotiation. Being able to maintain resourceful states, such as calmness and strength, will almost certainly be useful during negotiations, and being able to anchor and then fire states in your counter-party could be useful (see pages 148–149).

Perceptual positions (Chapter 11): This is an essential tool. Putting yourself in positions 2 and 3 before the negotiations will help inform you of the negotiation position and strategies of your counter-party. Sometimes it will be useful to create several position 2s, for example, different departments or individuals within your counter-party's organization, or your boss and his boss if you are going for a promotion. Perceptual positions will also be useful during the negotiation, perhaps by taking a brief pause to consider another perspective.

Values (Chapter 14): Understanding what is important to your counter-party regarding the topic being negotiated is essential. Though they may not be willing to divulge this, or even give you "misinformation" in a "combative" negotiation, you can use sensory acuity to notice whether certain topics or words seem to be more important than others, and use this information (even if it is more of a "guess") to test whether your ideas are correct. In a more congenial negotiation, for example, regarding your pay and workload, finding out what is important to your boss (or staff member) will be really useful.

Meta programs (Chapter 15): Patterns 1–7 are likely to be particularly important, and possibly the "Convincer" patterns (13 and 14). These will help you to present your arguments and suggestions in a way that is most likely to fit the needs and wants of the counter-party.

Handling objections and reframing (Chapter 12) and possibly Changing beliefs (Chapter 13): As with selling and procurement, in a "formal" negotiation situation, being able to reframe and handle objections will be essential. In a more informal negotiation, such as having received a job offer, it might be less important.

12. Presentations

Representational systems and predicates (Chapter 6): Remember to engage the senses, including the use of predicates from all four main representational systems. If, due to the nature of the topic, the audience is likely to show a preference for a particular representational system, concentrate a little more on that one compared to how you would if you were presenting to a more general audience.

- **Visual:** For example, show diagrams, videos, use PowerPoint or slides, use flip charts (neat writing, possibly different-colored pens) and, if possible, stick them to the wall during the presentation. Keep information on slides, etc. to a minimum and make sure that it is legible to people in the back row!

- **Auditory:** A presentation will almost always include words, so this will appeal to the auditory needs of the audience. If appropriate, use music or interviews, or videos with sound. Allow the audience the opportunity to speak, either to each other or to ask questions. To some extent, this latter element could be classed as kinesthetic, as it engages the audience and enables their participation.

- **Kinesthetic:** As well as the previous point, if appropriate, allow and encourage the audience to do an activity that relates to your topic. At the very least, make reference to, and/or ask them to consider (and possibly discuss in small groups), how the topic could affect them.

- **Auditory digital:** Provide relevant facts, figures, and evidence to support your points.

Submodalities (Chapter 9): If presenting is not an activity that appeals to you, you could alter your submodalities for presenting to be similar to those for a work activity that you do like.

Anchoring (Chapter 10): Use your resource anchor before and during the presentation if necessary. You can use spatial anchors for different points of the stage, and elicit states in the audience by using stories and metaphors (Chapter 7) and anchoring certain states in the audience (see Story 10.1 about anchoring laughter with gestures, page 155).

Perceptual positions (Chapter 11): You can use this to help you prepare the content of the presentation to suit the audience's wants and needs;

position 2 would be the audience, and position 3 would be a neutral observer. You could create several position 2s if there are different groups in the audience. You can also use perceptual positions to help you prepare for questions that the audience might ask.

Reframing and handling objections (Chapter 12) and possibly Changing beliefs (Chapter 13): Depending on the nature of the presentation, there might be objections or challenging questions from the audience, or you might be delivering negative information (e.g. bad financial results). Having the ability to put a positive spin at the right time(s) will help your presentation.

Language (Chapter 7): Sometimes being able to chunk up to a larger concept will enable you to handle objections and avoid getting bogged down in details. Being able to ask probing questions can engage or challenge the audience. Using stories and metaphors will help explain complex topics or illustrate points you want to make. Telling a story of how someone else (or another company) overcame a problem using the solution you are proposing can also help minimize resistance to your ideas.

Meta programs (Chapter 15): Many of the meta programs (especially 2 to 7) are on a spectrum. It will almost certainly be useful if you use language that appeals to both ends of the spectrum. Examples were given in some of the tips in Chapter 15. The "Frame of reference" filter will be particularly relevant to you when presenting to formal audiences, and/or to audiences who don't know you. Given that approximately one-third of people in the workplace are "internal" or "mainly internal," their natural tendency will be to decide for themselves who they will take seriously, so make sure that you introduce yourself and mention your credentials or relevant experience (see the tips for meta program 4 in Chapter 15).

In addition to these topics, here are some other elements of successful presentations.

- Prepare fully. Know your subject well, rehearse if appropriate, and get honest feedback before (and after) the presentation.
- If appropriate, use the 4-Mat system referred to in the segment on training earlier in this chapter (point 5).
- Remember that questions from the audience are simply questions, not heckles. Often they are simply requests for clarification or an explanation. Occasionally the person asking the

question might have an ulterior motive, such as "point-scoring," showing how knowledgeable they are or simply having a desire for attention. Even if a member of the audience is appearing to be a nuisance, remember the NLP Presupposition that everyone is doing the best they can with their current level of awareness while you respond appropriately.

Tip 17.1

View questions as an opportunity for you to clarify and give additional useful information to the whole audience, not just to the person asking the question. Also, when you have finished, ask the questioner if that answers their question, and use your sensory acuity to check whether "yes" really means "yes."

- Check all technology prior to the presentation and, where practical, have a backup plan.
- If it is a formal presentation, if possible visit or see the venue beforehand. This will help you visualize the presentation. Many of my clients do the mental-rehearsal exercise to help prepare for the presentation (see the "future pacing" segment on page 152). If you cannot see the venue before the day itself, arrive early to give yourself time to look at the venue and mentally rehearse.

13. Resolving conflicts and misunderstandings

Please remember that the following points are suggestions. You will need to use your common sense as each situation will be different. Also, if the conflict is between two other people, ask yourself whether the conflict is too strong for you to address given the level of experience you have.

Rapport (Chapter 5): This is particularly important, as being out of rapport will probably worsen the situation, whereas being in rapport will help smooth the potentially challenging moments.

Perceptual positions (Chapter 11): This is probably the key NLP technique to use: being able to see other perspectives before the situation escalates (or once it has become a conflict) will help prevent (or resolve) the situation. If you are acting as a mediator or coach, you could use the technique with each party separately, and once they have gained insight into the other person's perspective, you could then bring them together to take the situation forward (see Story 11.1 about the over-friendly director, page 165).

Values (Chapter 14): Conflicts are often caused by behaviors that transgress someone's values (the Neurological Levels model explains the link between values and behaviors). If you know what's important to someone and the criteria equivalents, you will already have an idea of what to do and what not to do to prevent conflicts. If a conflict or misunderstanding has arisen, by finding out which values have not been respected, you will be better able to manage or remedy the situation, whether you have been offended or whether you have offended someone else, or if you are "coaching" one of the parties. Remember, it is possible that the "offending party" did not realize the impact of their actions and that you might have distorted the meaning of the actual event (see the NLP Communication Model, Chapter 2).

Meta programs (Chapter 15): If you have certain meta-program preferences that are completely opposite, for example, to those of a colleague, you will probably be seeing a given situation in a very different way. For example, if you are very "toward" you may be annoyed at an "away from" colleague raising problems and concerns about a project that you think is a good idea (remember, your colleague may be annoyed at you too for being too optimistic!). By understanding meta programs, you will have a better insight into why someone else reacts the way they do, and into some ways to use language to influence them.

Anchoring (Chapter 10): Setting up and using a "calm" (or similar) anchor will help you be in the right state during the discussion about the situation.

14. Consultancy, including change management

Business consultancy can be used in most work-based activities. This section will cover the most relevant NLP techniques related to improving work processes and business reorganization.

Representational systems (Chapter 6): Story 6.2 (12 delegates at a conference advising a manager of a steel factory, page 85) describes how representational systems can be used to improve a business process by presenting information in a way that engages the main senses of the attendees.

Neurological Levels alignment (Chapter 8): The Neurological Levels model will help you structure the organizational-change process, considering the impact of the changes on each neurological level. You can also consider whether the organization is aligned (from a Neurological Levels perspective), for example, does its mission fit with its stated values and skillset (capabilities), and do the behaviors of management reflect the values espoused by management? Also, do all employees know and buy into the organization's mission and vision? (Remember the quote from the NASA janitor, page 123.)

Values (Chapter 14): Rarely will there be successful organizational change without addressing the organization's values. To some degree this is covered in the previous point.

Perceptual positions (Chapter 11): Consider the perspectives of the various groups affected by the business process or the proposed organizational changes. This might mean that there are several position 2s.

Meta programs (Chapter 15): As well as using the relevant influencing language, one particularly important meta program in the context of change-management and business-process consultancy is the "Relationship filter" ("sameness" and "difference," page 210). Most people do not like frequent or significant change and might feel uncomfortable about it. Wherever appropriate, remember to use "sameness with exception" influencing language with people who are at that end of the spectrum, pointing out how much will be the "same except" for certain changes, or "similar to" the way it was. You might even want to use terminology such as "enhancements" rather than "change."

15. Decision making

Strategies (Chapter 16): Identify your own decision-making strategy and make sure that you have sufficient information and opportunity to follow it.

Goal setting (Chapter 4): When making decisions, it is essential to know what you want to achieve so that the choices can be considered in that context. Even if it is not appropriate to create a full, well-formed outcome, many of the goal-setting questions will be relevant to your situation. Depending on the importance of the decision, asking the four ecology questions will be essential.

Neurological Levels (Chapter 8): As well as asking yourself the four ecology questions, you could consider the impact of the different choices on each of the levels.

Chunking (Chapter 7): Being able to chunk up to decide on the purpose of what it is that you are making a decision about and being able to chunk down to discuss the details and consequences of the decisions will usually help you make your decision.

Perceptual positions (Chapter 11): Being able to put yourself in the shoes of the various parties impacted by the decision will give you additional insight into making the best decision (this is what Carnegie was rumored to have done). This will involve your creating different position 2s to represent the relevant parties impacted by the decision.

Values (Chapter 14): If you need to make a choice regarding, for example, which computer system to buy, do the full values-elicitation process (steps 1–5) and, if necessary, elicit the criteria equivalents. Compare the alternatives to see which fulfill all the essential values (see Table 14.1).

16. Creative problem solving

Goal setting (Chapter 4): At the very least, know broadly what your desired outcome is. If it is relevant to the situation, spend time creating a well-formed (SMARTER) outcome, so that you are clear what the solution is aiming for.

Lateral chunking (Chapter 7): Lateral chunking will help you to think outside the box. You might find it useful to chunk up a couple of times before asking for different ways or different examples (the chunking-down questions).

Small words with big meanings (Chapter 7): Words such as "but," "however," and "although" might stifle creative thinking. Similarly, "or" might limit people to believing that there are only two options, when in reality there might be many more.

Anchoring (Chapter 10): Being in a suitable state, such as "creative" or "energized," might be useful for you and the other people involved in solving the problem. Using suitable music is a useful auditory anchor to create states.

Perceptual positions (Chapter 11): there are a couple of ways to use this technique. One option is to do a similar process to the one used by Walt Disney (page 166). Alternatively, use position 2 to represent the time in the future when you have resolved the problem, and position 3 to notice how you did it (this is explained on page 167 immediately after the Walt Disney example).

Reframing (Chapter 12): Reframing is about being able to turn negatives into positives or problems into opportunities. Being willing and able to think positively and reframe negatives are essential for creative problem solving.

Meta programs (Chapter 15): There are some meta programs that are more geared toward creative problem solving, for example, "options," "global," "differences," and "proactive." Therefore, choose people who exhibit a sufficient amount of these traits.

Summary

This chapter has indicated the key NLP techniques that would be useful in a wide variety of work activities and situations. Having read this chapter, you can refer to it when you would like a quick reminder of which NLP technique to use.

Suggested Answers to Exercises 7.2 and 7.4

Exercise 7.2 Linguistic presuppositions (page 102)

The main linguistic presuppositions are shown in brackets.

Good morning. Welcome to our third (ordinal) *annual* (time) *staff meeting. And the fact* (existence) *that there is such a big* (adjective) *turnout means* (equivalence) *that you're* (equivalence—the verb "to be") *all extremely* (adverb) *keen to take the organization forward to the next level* (existence and adjective—"the next level"). *The main* (adjective) *reason we're all here is* (equivalence) *so that we can* (possibility) *look for* (awareness—"look") *even better ways to do this after* (time) *last year's great* (adjective) *improvement. And we have to* (necessity) *move forward, because* (causation—"because") *standing still means* (equivalence) *falling behind our competitors. And whether we move forward quickly or* (or) *slightly* (adverb) *less quickly, our aim has to* (necessity) *be focused* (awareness) *on our success* (existence), *and on becoming number one* (ordinal).

Exercise 7.4 Abstract language (page 111)

The main Milton Model patterns are shown in brackets.

Good morning. Thank you all (universal) *for coming. Some of you have travelled a long distance, some a shorter distance* (presuppositions), *to be here on time* (pacing). *I guess you're probably wondering* (assumption) *why I asked you to come here on this sunny morning. And it's good* (impersonal judgment) *that you're wondering* (assumption, unspecified verb), *because* (causation) *this curiosity is* (equivalence) *the basis of how we can* (possibility) *move forward to achieve the success and excellence* (frozen verbs) *that we all* (universal) *want to achieve* (assumption). *We all* (universal) *want more* (unspecified comparison) *success and to be happy* (simple deletion), *don't we?* (inserted question) *And that's good* (impersonal judgment), *because* (causation) *in this economic environment we need* (necessity) *to progress* (unspecified verb)*; people* (unspecified person) *expect it; successful companies never* (universal) *stand still* (impossible behavior—can a company stand?)*; successful companies keep looking* (impossible behavior—can a company look?) *for ways forward.*

Choosing an NLP Training Course

This appendix outlines the range of NLP training courses available to you should you wish to learn about NLP in a live training environment. This range extends from introductory, non-certificated workshops through to the highest level of qualification in the NLP field, Master Trainer.

Background

It is important to be aware that there are different approaches to training NLP. There are several NLP "bodies" and there are some significant variations between them in terms of:

- Style of delivery of training.
- Approach to ethics and ecology.
- Length of training required for certification.
- Course syllabus.
- The number of trainers required to certify students.

At the time of writing, there is no unique set of standards or governing body, although there is a recognition amongst several of the leading NLP bodies worldwide of the need for collaboration in setting standards.

This appendix initially describes non-certificated courses and then briefly describes the various courses that lead to a qualification.

Introduction courses and other non-certificated courses

Introduction courses typically range from a half day through to two days and can be general courses or specialize in specific areas, for example, NLP for selling or NLP for managers.

Other non-certificated courses may be longer and go into more depth about a particular aspect of NLP, for example, NLP and sport, or modeling using NLP. Often these courses are for people with some previous NLP training and this is usually made clear in the course-marketing material.

Certificated courses

There are five main levels of certification. In order of hierarchy these are:

- Diploma.
- Practitioner.
- Master Practitioner.
- Trainer.
- Master Trainer.

Neither Diploma nor Practitioner courses require any previous NLP experience, whereas the other three levels require delegates to be certified to the previous level. When thinking about the different levels of qualification, you might find it useful to bear in mind the three key benefits of NLP described in Chapter 1:

- Improving communication.
- Changing thinking, attitudes, behaviors, and beliefs.
- Replicating excellence.

NLP Diploma

Diploma courses last 20–30 hours, normally over three or four days, and include most of the topics covered in the first 12 chapters (apart from most of Chapter 7 on language, which is left to Practitioner level) and in Chapter 14. The topics are not always covered in as much depth as in this book. These courses are useful for people who want to gain a solid grounding in improving communication and in some of the aspects of changing behaviors. These courses are mainly aimed at people who want to use NLP to help themselves, and possibly colleagues, deal with relatively minor challenges. Some NLP training businesses treat the Diploma as a foundation for the NLP Practitioner course.

NLP Practitioner

Although there are many differences in the duration and structure of Practitioner courses, the content of courses is broadly similar in that they cover most of the Diploma content—more of the techniques for changing behaviors and beliefs, and further language skills. Because of the different durations and structures of Practitioner courses, the practitioners from these courses will have varying degrees of ability and experience in dealing with situations and challenges faced by their clients, should they wish to use NLP in a business coaching or consulting capacity.

If you choose to become an NLP Practitioner, make sure that the course suits your requirements (some sources of information to help you choose the right NLP course are provided at the end of this appendix, together with a brief summary of the points).

Equally, if you are using the services of an NLP Practitioner at work, you might wish to ensure that they are suitably trained and qualified to meet your requirements.

NLP Master Practitioner

Master Practitioner courses build on the content taught at Practitioner level (Practitioner certification is a prerequisite for Master Practitioner courses) and cover new material regarding communication and language, changing behaviors and beliefs, and modeling. These courses usually provide deeper levels of personal development; the courses broaden and deepen students' capability to facilitate "change work" with other people.

Though the syllabus of Practitioner courses is relatively similar across the different NLP training bodies, the content of Master Practitioner is more varied. As with Practitioner courses, Master Practitioners will have different degrees of ability and experience depending on the type of course they have attended. Similar considerations apply for choosing a Master

Practitioner course as for choosing a Practitioner course, and for organizations using the services of NLP Master Practitioners.

It is important to note that although Practitioners and Master Practitioners may run training courses and workshops, only Certified Trainers are able to certify students as Diploma holders, Practitioners, or Master Practitioners.

NLP Trainer and Master Trainer

NLP Trainers have met the criteria of a Certified Trainers' training which is open only to Master Practitioners. They are able to certify people at the level of Diploma, Practitioner, and Master Practitioner. Trainers' training courses will vary in terms of content and duration, typically ranging from seven days to 19 days, including evaluation. Generally, an effective NLP Trainers' training course will:

- Teach students how to run NLP courses and how to teach and certify at NLP Diploma, Practitioner, and Master Practitioner level.
- Teach students excellent presentation skills.
- Thoroughly test their knowledge of NLP.

A typical and thorough evaluation process lasts three to four days.

Normally, to become a Master Trainer, you will have been a Certified Trainer for several years, have run several Practitioner and Master Practitioner courses, and have made a significant contribution to the NLP field. Only Master Trainers can certify NLP Trainers and other Master Trainers.

Summary of considerations
when choosing a course

Whichever type of course you choose, it is recommended that you satisfy yourself that the course will provide you with what you want from it. Here are some considerations you might want to take into account:

- Reputation and qualifications of the trainer(s).
- Duration of the course.

- Style of the course (such as modular or block, pre-course study or all face to face).
- Number of qualified assistants available to answer questions, observe, and give feedback during exercises.
- Standing of the body/board that recognizes the course.
- Pass rate (if everyone always passes, what is the qualification worth?).
- Process and standards for certification.
- Size of the training course (5, 50, or 500 delegates?).
- Follow-up support available.
- Specialist subjects covered by the course (such as sport, business, personal development, health).
- Number of trainers required to certify students (many schools specify two).

Both *www.thelazarus.com* and *www.anlp.org* contain free guides to choosing an NLP course. (The Association of NLP is the main NLP body in the UK.)

Contact the author or visit *www.thelazarus.com* for further details and updated information about NLP training and the different certificated courses available.

Resources for Further Learning

Books

Coaching

Downey, Miles, *Effective Coaching* (Orion Publishing, 1999).

Landsberg, Max, *The Tao of Coaching* (HarperCollins, 1997).

McLeod, Angus, *Performance Coaching* (Crown House, 2003).

Whitmore, John, *Coaching for Performance: GROWing human potential and purpose* (4th edition, Nicholas Brealey Publishing, 2009).

General

Covey, Stephen R. *The 7 Habits of Highly Effective People: Powerful Lesson in Personal Change* (Simon & Schuster, 1992).

Csikszentmihalyi, Mihaly, *Flow: The classic work on how to achieve happiness* (Rider (Random House), 2002).

Festinger, Leon, *A Theory of Cognitive Dissonance* (Stanford University Press, 1957).

Navarro, Joe with Karlins, Martin, *What every BODY is saying: an ex-FBI agent's guide to speed-reading people* (HarperCollins Publishers, 2008).

Pink, Daniel, *Drive: The Surprising Truth About What Motivates Us* (Canongate Books, 2010).

Rodgers, Everett M. *Diffusions of Innovation* (The Free Press (Simon & Schuster) 2003).

Meta programs and values

Charvet, Shelle Rose, *Words That Change Minds: Mastering the Language of Infl uence* (Kendall/Hunt Publishing, 1995).

Hall, L. Michael and Bodenhamer, Bob, *Figuring Out People: Design Engineering With Meta-Programs* (Crown House Publishing, 1997).

James, Tad and Woodsmall, Wyatt, *Time Line Therapy and the Basis of Personality* (Meta Publications, 1988) (Sections III and IV only).

Metaphors

Lawley, James and Tompkins, Penny, *Metaphors in Mind* (The Developing Company Press, 2000).

Rosen, Sidney, *My Voice Will Go With You: The Teaching Tales of Milton H. Erickson* (W. W. Norton & Co., 1982).

Meta-Model language

Bandler, Richard and Grinder, John, *The Structure of Magic, Volume I* (Science and Behaviour Books Inc., 1975).

"Milton Model" language

Bandler, Richard and Grinder, John, *Patterns of the Hypnotic Techniques of Milton H. Erickson, MD, Volume 1* (Meta Publications, 1975).

Bandler, Richard and Grinder, John, *Patterns of the Hypnotic Techniques of Milton H. Erickson, MD, Volume 2* (Meta Publications, 1975).

Moine, Donald J. and Lloyd, Kenneth, *Unlimited Selling Power: How to Master Hypnotic Selling Skills* (Prentice Hall, 1990). (Also useful for selling.)

Negotiating

Thompson, Leigh, *The Truth About Negotiations* (Pearson Education Ltd., 2008).

NLP: Belief change and handling objections

Dilts, Robert, *Changing Belief Systems with NLP* (Meta Publications, 1990).

Dilts, Robert, *Sleight of Mouth: The Magic of Conversational Belief Change* (Meta Publications, 1999).

NLP: Coaching

O'Connor, Joseph and Lages, Andrea, *Coaching With NLP: A practical guide to getting the best out of yourself and others* (Element (HarperCollins), 2004).

NLP: General

Bodenhamer, Bob and Hall, L. Michael, *The User's Manual For The Brain, Volume I* and *Volume II* (Crown House Publishing, 1999 and 2003 respectively).

Dilts, Robert and DeLozier, Judith, *Encyclopaedia of Neuro- Linguistic Programming and NLP New Coding* (NLP University Press, 2000). (See "Websites" on page 277.)

O'Connor, Joseph, *NLP Workbook: a practical guide to achieving the results you want* (Element (HarperCollins), 2001).

Wake, Lisa, *NLP: Principles in Practice* (Ecademy Press, 2010).

NLP: Modeling

Dilts, Robert, *Modelling with NLP* (Meta Publications, 1998).

NLP: Selling

Johnson, Kerry L., *Selling with NLP* (Nicholas Brealey Publishing, 1994).

O'Connor, Joseph and Prior, Robin, *Successful Selling With NLP: Powerful ways to help you connect with your customers* (Thorsons (HarperCollins), 1995).

NLP: Strategies

Dilts, Robert, Grinder, John, Bandler, Richard and DeLozier, Judith, *Neuro-Linguistic Programming: Volume 1, The Study of Subjective Experience* (Meta Publications, 1980).

Personality traits (Myers–Briggs Type Indicator)

Keirsey, David and Bates, Marilyn, *Please Understand Me: Character & Temperament Types* (Prometheus Nemesis Book Company Ltd., 1984).

Submodalities

Andreas, Steve and Andreas, Connirae, *Change Your Mind And Keep The Change* (Real People Press, 1987).

Bandler, Richard, *Using Your Brain For A Change* (Real People Press, 1985).

Also available from the author

Successful NLP: For the results you want (Crimson Publishing, 2010).

The Little NLP Workbook (Crimson Publishing, 2012).

The NLP Pocket Handbook An 84-page, A6 guide to the NLP Practitioner and Master Practitioner material. Available from *www.thelazarus.com*.

Ahead of the Game: How to use your mind to win in sport (Ecademy Press, 2006).

Audio and visual material

There are several providers of NLP-related audio material ranging from one or two topics through to Practitioner-level and Master Practitioner-level CD sets.

Available from the author

There are the following CDs available from The Lazarus Consultancy Ltd., covering most of the topics contained in this book.

NLP Practitioner CD Series: *A 16-CD set, lasting approximately 1 1/2 hours, with a fully referenced training manual. This comprises the pre-study material for The Lazarus Consultancy Fast-Track NLP Practitioner Course.*

Understanding, Predicting and Influencing Behaviour—4 CD Series: *A 4-CD set, lasting 4 1/2 hours, covering the values and deep filters referred to in this book plus many more, with a fully referenced manual.*

Understanding, Predicting and Influencing Behaviour—6 CD NLP Series: *The same as the 4-CD set above, plus two additional CDs covering how to change values and deep filters. For that reason, this set is relevant only to NLP Practitioners and Master Practitioners.*

There is a growing amount of video material available on the Internet, ranging from demonstrations of techniques through to discussions and interviews about NLP-related topics.

Websites

There are numerous NLP Websites; most NLP training schools and NLP bodies will have websites, which they frequently update. NLP University's Website (*www.nlpu.com*) contains an electronic version of the *Encyclopaedia of Neuro-Linguistic Programming and NLP New Coding*, and free searches of 25 items per day are allowed.

Glossary

Anchor: A representation/stimulus connected to and triggering a subsequent response. Anchors can be naturally occurring or set up deliberately.

Associated: The memory of an experience as if seen through your own eyes (i.e. re-living it).

At Cause: Having a positive, can-do attitude, as opposed to *At Effect*.

At Effect: Having a negative, complaining attitude, as opposed to *At Cause*.

Auditory digital (Ad): The *representational system* dealing with logic and the way we talk to ourselves.

Beliefs: *Generalizations* we make about the world and our opinions about it. They form the rules about what we can and cannot do.

Calibration: The ability to notice and measure changes with respect to a standard. Usually involves the comparison between two different sets of external, non-verbal cues for a particular person, such as breathing rate or eye focus.

Chunking: Changing a perception by moving a "chunk," or a group of bits of information, in the direction of more abstraction, or more detail, or laterally, through the use of language.

Collapsing anchors: An NLP technique to remove the impact of a negative anchor. See also *Anchor*.

Communication Model: See *NLP Communication Model*.

Content reframe: See *Meaning reframe*.

Context: The particular setting or situation in which the content occurs.

Context reframe: Giving another meaning to a statement by changing the context.

Criteria: See *Values.*

Criteria equivalent: The equivalent of a value; how someone would know that their value/criteria has been met.

Cross-over matching: *Matching* one aspect of a person's external behavior or physiology with a different physiological movement.

Deep filter: See *Meta programs.*

Deletion: Deletion occurs when we leave out a portion of our experience as we make our *internal representations.*

Dissociated: The memory of an experience, seeing your whole body in the picture.

Distortion: Distortion occurs when something is mistaken for that which it is not, or when things that have not occurred are included in our *internal representations.*

Driver: The *submodality* that makes the most difference in our meaning of an experience.

Ecology: The study of the consequences, or results, or impact, of any change that occurs on the wider system.

First position: This is one of the *perceptual positions.* First position is when you are seeing a situation from your own point of view.

Future pace: Mentally rehearsing a future result, usually immediately after an NLP intervention.

Generalization: Generalization occurs when one specific experience represents, or is generalized to, a whole class of experiences.

Hierarchy of Ideas: The level of abstraction of ideas and concepts, ranging from abstract to specific. The Hierarchy of Ideas can also be used for lateral thinking.

Internal representations: The content of our thinking or the confirmation of information that includes pictures, sounds, feelings, tastes, smells, and self-talk.

Leading: Changing your own behavior with enough rapport so that another person will follow.

Linguistic presupposition: The linguistic equivalent of assumptions, that is, what is presumed by the words someone uses (they are a completely different topic from the *NLP Presuppositions*).

Matching: Replicating, to some degree, one or more aspects of a person's physiology or voice.

Meaning reframe: Giving another meaning to a statement by considering other (more positive) possible meanings (sometimes called a *content reframe*).

Meta Model: A model of language, derived from the work of Virginia Satir, that gives us an "overview" of language. It allows us to recognize *deletions*, *generalizations*, and *distortions* in our language and gives us questions to clarify imprecise language and gain specificity.

Meta programs: These are unconscious, content-free programs we run that filter our experiences (sometimes referred to as *deep filters* in this book).

Milton Model: A set of language patterns used by Milton Erickson. These patterns use language in an abstract way, so that people can create their own meaning from the Milton Model patterns used.

Mirroring: Reflecting the physiology of someone as if looking into a mirror.

Modalities: Refers to our internal representations, which relate to the five senses (*visual*, *auditory*, *kinesthetic*, *olfactory*, *gustatory*) and also our internal dialogue.

Modeling: Modeling is the process by which all of NLP was created. In modeling, we elicit what someone does, in their mind and physiologically, that allows them to produce a certain behavior. Then we codify these actions in a series of steps designed to make the behavior easy to reproduce.

Neurological Levels: A model frequently used in NLP to classify our thinking and situations into the following categories: environment; behaviors; capabilities; beliefs and values; identity; and purpose/mission. The model is sometimes known as *logical levels*.

NLP Communication Model: A model of how people internally process external events and how this internal processing impacts on behaviors and results.

NLP Presuppositions: See *Presuppositions of NLP*.

Pacing: Gaining and maintaining rapport with another person over a period of time by *matching* or *mirroring* their external behavior and/or voice.

Perceptual positions: Describes points of view in a specific situation: *first position* is our own point of view; *second position* is usually someone else's point of view; *third position* is the point of view of a dissociated observer—much like an overview.

Predicates: Words and phrases that often presuppose one of the *representational systems*.

Preferred representational system: This is the *representational system* that someone most often uses to think and to organize their experiences. This is the representational system that we commonly and most easily employ.

Presuppositions of NLP: Assumptions or convenient beliefs, which are not necessarily "true" but which, if accepted and believed, will change our thinking and improve our results.

Principles for Success: These are six principles which, when adhered to, increase our chances of success, both for individual tasks and in life generally.

Rapport: The ability to relate to others in a way that creates a climate of trust and understanding.

Reframing: The process of making a shift in the nature of a problem, or changing the structure or context of a statement, to give it another meaning.

Representational system: This is the way we code sensory information and experience our world. There is a representational system for each of our senses.

Resources: Resources are the means to create change within oneself or to accomplish an outcome. Resources might include certain states or adopting specific physiology.

Resourceful state: This refers to any state where a person has positive, helpful emotions available to them and is operating from them behaviorally.

Second position: Relating to a *perceptual position*. Second position is the point of view of the other person(s) involved in the situation.

Sensory acuity: The ability to notice and gain awareness of another person's conscious and subconscious responses through their physiology and/or voice.

State: Our internal emotional condition.

Strategies: A series and sequence of internal and external representations that lead to a specific result.

Submodalities: These are fine distinctions (or the subsets of the *modalities* V, A, K, O, G, and Ad) that are part of each *representational system* and which encode and give meaning to our experiences.

Third position: Relating to a *perceptual position*. Third position is the point of view of a dissociated observer, an overview.

Values: Criteria that are important to you, what you look for, or want, in something. See also *Criteria*.

Well-formed conditions: Well-formed conditions allow us to specify outcomes that are more achievable, because the way the goal is set conforms to certain rules/principles.

Well-formed outcomes: These are goals and outcomes that are stated and set in a way that meets those of *well-formed conditions*.

About the Author

Jeremy Lazarus is a certified Master Trainer of NLP, and an Accredited Master Executive Coach. He qualified as an NLP Practitioner in 1999 and as a Master Practitioner and Trainer in 2000. He specializes in the applications of NLP in the workplace and in sport.

Jeremy is the director of The Lazarus Consultancy Ltd., a London-based coaching and training business which has coached and trained entrepreneurs, SMEs, the National Health Service, and blue-chip organizations. He has also worked with several elite athletes and sports coaches, including Premier League football clubs and the Great Britain pistol shooting team. Jeremy is a guest lecturer at two UK universities.

Prior to starting The Lazarus Consultancy Ltd. in 1999, he had a successful career in finance as an accountant, management consultant, corporate treasurer, and finance director. He originally qualified as an accountant and corporate treasurer.

He has written three other best-selling books on NLP:

- *Ahead of the Game: How to Use Your Mind to Win in Sport* (Ecademy Press)
- *Successful NLP: for the results you want* (Crimson Publishing)
- *The Little NLP Workbook* (Crimson Publishing)